READY TO RISE

ONE MAN'S JOURNEY FROM PARALYSIS TO LIBERATION

EUGENE TEJADA WITH MARK CHAN

Ready to Rise
Copyright © 2020 by Eugene Tejada with Mark Chan

All rights reserved. No part of this publication may be reproduced, distributed, or transmitted in any form or by any means, including photocopying, recording, or other electronic or mechanical methods, without the prior written permission of the author, except in the case of brief quotations embodied in critical reviews and certain other non-commercial uses permitted by copyright law.

Tellwell Talent
www.tellwell.ca

ISBN
978-0-2288-3281-2 (Paperback)
978-0-2288-3282-9 (eBook)

TABLE OF CONTENTS

Foreword by Jimmy Alapag v
Chapter 1   "Even Keel" 1
Chapter 2   "The Perils of Fame" 10
Chapter 3   "Absolute Power" 20
Chapter 4   "Multiple Masks Part I" 28
Chapter 5   "Multiple Masks Part II" 36
Chapter 6   "Daddy's Boy" 45
Chapter 7   "Back to Life" 55
Chapter 8   "Friends and Foes" 74
Chapter 9   "Risk Averse" 82
Chapter 10 "Better Skilled Than Safe" 90
Chapter 11 "Friends in High Places" 98
Chapter 12 "The Four Words" 109
Chapter 13 "Facets of Forgiveness" 116
Chapter 14 "A Lover's Kiss" 123
Chapter 15 "Closing with Thanks" 134

FOREWORD BY JIMMY ALAPAG

I still remember this day so clearly. I had just arrived home from practice and was in the shower, while my girlfriend (and now wife of almost 10 years, LJ) and her little brother were downstairs. All of a sudden, I could hear footsteps sprinting up the stairs as LJ's brother burst through the door. He immediately shouted: "turn on the TV, Kuya (big brother in Tagalog)! Gene is on the court! He's not moving!" LJ's brother had spoken so fast that I didn't quite understand what he said. As I was asking about what happened, he ran toward my TV and turned it to the live Philippine Basketball Association game between the Purefoods Chunkee Giants and the Red Bull Barako. There lying underneath the basket, responsive but motionless from the neck down, was my friend and brother Eugene Tejada.

Gene and I came to Manila in 2003 with many of the same hopes and dreams. We did this to become pro basketball players in the PBA, make our impact on the league, and inspire others through our experiences. I had come to Manila before that in 2002, but after my brief stint with the National Team ended abruptly due to injury, I found myself back in the US. It was back to the grind for the next few months, as I prepared for a return to Manila for the PBA draft. Gene and I had crossed paths a few times in the US during the competitive Filipino-American tournaments that were once a hotbed for Filipino players looking for a chance to make it to the PBA. Those tournaments were highly competitive, and some of the bet who played would later make their attempts at a PBA career in Manila as well. After the disappointment of my injury, I eventually made my way back to Manila for the 2003 PBA draft. Together with Gene and Harvey Carey, an old college rival in the States, we began workouts with various PBA teams, doing our best to leave lasting impressions on teams leading up to the draft.

January 12, 2003 was a dream come true for all of us. Gene, Harvey and I were all selected amongst the top 15 picks of the PBA draft. Our pro journey had begun. I remember how special it was to be able to go through that rookie season together. Although Harvey and I played together at Talk N Text while Gene was with Alaska, that didn't stop us from spending countless hours together off the court. Being away from family is a big adjustment for any aspiring player hoping to make it in the PBA, and we were no different. Back in those days when high-speed internet was not around, much less any social media outlets, our spare time was usually spent eating out or being at each other's places to play Sony PlayStation. I come from a family with 5 siblings, so travelling across the world to chase a childhood dream, leaving the comforts of a supportive, tight-knit family to start a new chapter of my life abroad was far from easy. But that's what made my friendship with Gene and Harvey so special. To this day, we are still very much the best of friends. No matter what experiences we encountered as rookies, there was comfort knowing the support we had for each other was strong. Twenty years later, the gratitude I have for our friendship and brotherhood runs deep, because without this friendship, I know I would have never made it through our first year in Manila.

There are so many memorable stories to share about our experiences through the years—I could probably start a book about them, but they are for another time. One story, however, still brings me a lot of laughs to this day. To celebrate our official entry into the PBA together, we decided we would step out into the Manila nightlife scene. There was never a shortage of places to go, especially for 3 young, single pro basketball players. Gene had just bought a new car because up to that point, we were just taking taxis to get around Manila just to get to practice and anywhere else we needed to go. We set off that night and visited some of the local hotspots, and safe to say, we had a great time! But as we made our way home in the early hours of the morning, driving along EDSA (the main highway in Manila), we felt a slight bump on the road. We didn't think it was anything at the time but moments later, we realized Gene's car had a flat tire. So there we were, three newly-drafted PBA rookies on EDSA with a flat tire on a new car. We had absolutely no idea who we had to call or how we were going to get help, and the humidity of the Manila air made it feel like it was 200 degrees outside. It took us what seemed like an eternity just to locate where the spare tire was, because none of us could also find the new car's manual. Eventually, about an hour later, our hands and clothes were soaked in a mixture of sweat and black tire residue. We got the tire changed and made our way home safely, albeit much dirtier than when we left. Our first night out as professional athletes was officially in the books!

As Gene lay on the court that night on Mother's Day, 2006, the first person I reached out to was Harvey. He was already on his way to the hospital, so I immediately got dressed and rushed out the door. So many thoughts ran through my mind as I sped to the hospital. Why Gene? He was a pro athlete who had just turned the corner in his career, and he was definitely on his way to making an impact in the PBA. I had so many questions raging inside my head as I drove to see my friend in the hospital. Would he be okay? Would he get back on his feet again and play the game of basketball just once more? These were all questions I did not have the answers to and so I took a brief moment to pray in the car, asking God to watch over Gene as I arrived at the hospital.

A large crowd of people gathered at the Emergency room. Our circle of friends had heard the news and they had also rushed to the hospital to show their support. I didn't know what to say in the brief first moment that I saw Gene. He was being wheeled in from the ambulance to be taken to the Emergency Room. So many more tests and X-rays awaited, and I could see the worry in his eyes. The only thing that came to my mind at the time was to tell him that I loved him, that I was praying for him, and that I would be there to support him in any way I could. It was so hard in that moment to accept the reality that my brother Gene, someone who still had so much promise in his career, was likely never going to be able to play basketball ever again. What I didn't see in that moment was that God had other plans for him. These were plans that were going to lead him to inspire and impact people far beyond the lines of the basketball court.

The next few months of Gene's recovery were some of the most arduous moments I have ever seen anyone go through. To see Gene and his daily struggle with many of the simple things we often take for granted in life was truly difficult. But what I also witnessed in those early months was Gene's sheer will, determination, and heart to defy the odds in order to get back on his feet and walk again. As you go on to read this book, I hope Gene's story touches your life like it has mine. I stand here today proud to call Eugene Tejada my friend and brother. To watch someone you love fight through insurmountable odds, yet still be here today to tell his amazing story is only possible by God's grace. I am so thankful he has put his heartfelt thoughts into this book.

To my guy Gene, a loving father and devoted husband—thank you for being such an inspiration in my life and in the lives of many others. Through all of the hills and valleys life has brought you through, your incredible story resonates more than any winning rebound our three-point shot could ever have. I hope those who read your story see the beauty in your struggles, share in the joy of your successes, and feel the impact that God's love and guidance has had on your life. Continue to inspire the world, my brother, one step at a time!

CHAPTER 1

"EVEN KEEL"

It was Mother's Day, 2006 and I was exactly where I wanted to be. After languishing on the bench of the Alaska Aces for the first three years of my career, I had played my way onto the roster of Purefoods, one of the best franchises in the PBA--the Philippine Basketball Association. With a condor's wingspan and a great motor, I wreaked defensive havoc as a forward and was tough to keep off the boards. I'd inherited my athleticism and my height (6'4") from my father, a former PBA player, and now I was putting it to good use. This was my time. The world was my oyster. It didn't even matter that my contract as a professional basketball player was expiring because I was at the top of my game, on the court and off.

I had everything a person could want: an amazing job for which I was paid lots of money to play the game I loved and a girlfriend whose appearances in men's magazines made me the envy of other males in the Philippines. I had a bit of fame and adulation, not necessarily Hollywood Movie Star level fame, but enough that people gawked when I walked around the streets of Manila. Although it had felt awkward at first, I was beginning to enjoy being stopped by fans who wanted to have their picture taken with me. *I could get used to this* was a thought that had started to play in my mind repeatedly.

Then, Mother's Day and what was supposed to be a routine play in a game that was part of the regular season. A win would have given us an advantage in the playoffs but we were being blown out by a Red Bull team that was hungry and in contention. I was coming back from an ankle injury and wasn't even supposed to play but my coach, Ryan Gregorio, asked if I would like some court time to, you know, "work out some of the kinks." The warrior and competitor in me said yes so there I was, playing my heart out, while the rest of the athletes were playing out the string.

My teammate, Roger Yap, dove the lane for a shot that he would miss. Being a tenacious rebounder and the team's resident "garbage cleaner," a title of honor in professional basketball describing a player who goes after every loose ball as if their life depends on it, I followed the ball. I rose for the offensive rebound and might have been successful in doing so had contact from behind not thrown me off-balance. I landed on the floor expecting a little jarring, totally unaware of what was about to hit me.

You see, the player behind me was a 6'9" mountain named Mick Pennisi who played for the Red Bull team. Weighing between 220 and 250 pounds, he too had been knocked off balance and was about to come down on me, full force, as I lay on the floor. The impact of Pennisi's body hitting my neck fractured my C5 and C6 vertebrae. Immediately I felt an unnatural jolt of electricity in my body, as if I had been struck by lightning.

The shock of the impact threw my system into overdrive. My feet felt like they were my hands. My upper limbs seemed to be all the way down by my legs. My brain struggled to make sense of what had happened. With crucial connections lost, everything was upside down. I lay on the floor of the Ynares Center in the Philippines on that cold and wet day in May and I knew my career was over.

By some strange coincidence, I had been reading actor Christopher Reeve's biography around that time and was familiar with the horseback riding accident that had left him paralyzed. His story came to me in those moments following the incident. Based on what I had read and learned from Reeve's book, I knew I was in real trouble. I lay on the floor for what seemed to be an eternity and thought about the odds of this happening to me. It was as if I had won the lottery, only in reverse. Why now? Why me?

∗∗∗

People talk about the "Good Life." They talk about being handed a "golden ticket." But they also talk about being careful what you wish for. In 2016, *Time Magazine* ran a story about people who had won the lottery but later regretted their windfall.[1] A Virginia man named Jack Whittaker who was interviewed for the article claimed a $315 million jackpot but later said, "I wish I had torn the ticket up."

He was robbed of $545,000 while sitting in a car outside a strip club and later attributed the death of his granddaughter directly to winning the big prize. Perhaps the most disturbing part of the magazine article concerning Mr. Whittaker was towards the end when Whittaker stated, "I just don't like Jack Whittaker…I don't like what I've become."

Also featured in the piece was Abraham Shakespeare from Florida who won $30 million in 2009 at the age of 47 but later claimed, "I'd have been better off broke." He ended up shot twice in the chest and buried under a slab of concrete. Other winners have lamented the way they instantly became seen as a meal ticket by those around them following their lucky wins. "People who you've loved deep down…(turn) into vampires trying to suck the life out of (you)," was the way Sandra Hayes described it. She was a Missouri lottery winner who took a prize of $224 million in 2006 that she had to split with a dozen coworkers. Hayes ended up writing a book about how the lottery had negatively impacted her life and she attributed a lot of the stress of winning to the emotional pain caused by the greed of the people she once considered close to her heart.

Three different people with the three different stories about how the supposed "good life" can turn sour. These cautionary tales provide us with a glimpse of all the bad things that can happen even when you're expecting nothing but good. The stories reflect a perspective that I have become all too familiar with in my own life: not everything that glitters is gold.

Of course, I didn't actually win the lottery but, if one were to compute the odds of getting hurt the way that I did, they'd probably be even greater than the chances of winning the lottery in my home state. And just as those lottery winners found that their "good luck" had unexpected negative consequences, I found myself surprised to discover that being paralyzed had a profoundly positive effect on my life.

A number of things had to break "bad" in order for me to reach the conclusion that my paralysis had a silver lining even if I had lost millions in potential career earnings along with the ability to walk. Things have a

---

[1] Melissa Chan, "Here's How Winning the Lottery Makes You Miserable." *Time Magazine.* Jan 12th, 2016.

funny way of working themselves out. When the prominent woman I was dating left me, I was devastated at first, so much so that I actually thought about killing myself. It turned out to be the best thing for me, however. It allowed me to reconnect with the love of my life, Andrea, an intelligent, loving woman and successful manager moving up the corporate ladder. At the time of writing this, we have been married for five years and it's a triple win for me in this category because Andrea gave birth to twin boys and we are now a loving family.

When my career ended and I left the shores of Manila, it felt like a failure but Manila had been a place that, for all intents and purposes, had been toxic for me. I loved being asked for autographs and I relished the feeling of people wanting to have their picture taken with me but, deep inside, I knew this lifestyle was harmful. My ego grew as did the psychological need to be the center of attention. I had a strong sense of entitlement and was beginning to feel as if the world revolved around me--or at least I felt it should. Being paralyzed initiated the transition away from a destructive lifestyle of partying and alcohol and the constant craving for the company of women--it's hard for a quadriplegic to play the role of lothario.

I abandoned the "rock star" lifestyle I had been living for a quieter world at home and was able to grow into a better, more authentic version of myself. Even if there are days where my twin boys take up so much of my time and energy that there is little left over to do the things I want to do for myself, I would rather have *this* than whatever it was I had before. And I only have to think about how doctors back in Manila would have considered it a major medical miracle for me to even have children after my paralysis to remember how truly fortunate I am to have been blessed with these boys, no matter how rowdy they get.

Another aspect of that silver lining is that, perhaps as expected, I had the opportunity to find out who my true friends were during those difficult months following my injury. After an initial honeymoon period full of sympathy and concern, my old crowd began to drift away. Newspaper headlines no longer blared my name and the television news stories grew shorter before finally stopping entirely just like the visits my so-called friends made to my bedside in the hospital. Apparently, there really isn't much social leverage one can get from being friends with a paralytic. My injury became a sort of litmus test that revealed which of my friends would be part of a solid base of support and which of them were acid.

In the years since then, I have had the opportunity to do a lot of reading. At some point, I came across the writings of Vilfredo Pareto. Pareto, an Italian engineer, sociologist, economist, political scientist, and philosopher believed that 80% of a person's productivity will come from 20% of their work. Pareto may have observed this distribution in the field of economics but I noticed that his principle applied to the quality of my friendships.

I experienced a great loss when 80% of my so-called friends left me but, in hindsight, that may have been one of the best things that happened to me. I developed stronger relationships with the 20% that stuck with me throughout and received greater emotional reward from those stalwarts than I ever had from the many who abandoned me. These loyal friends have made all the difference in my life. I am no Sandra Hayes whose lottery friends were like vampires sucking the blood out of her.

But before you get out the violins or the wooden stakes, I must confess that I played my part in creating these blood-sucking friendships. I took from others as much as they took from me. Everyone was a means to an end. If someone could not help me in my quest to become the best player in the PBA, or at least the most notorious, I had little use for them. I made a habit of treating certain people small while treating others, those who could enrich my social network, way too big. It came back to me in spades when these "friends" left me during my darkest days but their disappearance opened a door for the true companions to step through and it paved the road to being a better friend myself.

Last in my tally of what this strange reverse lottery has given me is a new sense of self. My identity, my very idea of who I was, had always been firmly rooted in basketball. It was the one thing I was good at. I hated school and attended classes only because I had to do well enough academically to qualify to put on a jersey. By the time I became a professional player, I was basing my entire self-worth on how well I was doing on the court.

During my first few years in the PBA, playing for a team called the Alaska Aces, I was the lowest man on the totem pole. The coaches and my teammates made fun of the way I played, the way I shot the ball, and sometime just my appearance. They compared me to the goofy character

Jim in the movie *American Pie*. I felt a deep shame throughout my rookie season as insecurities from my struggles with a learning disability began to resurface. Once the butt of jokes in the classroom, I was once again the one being laughed at during practices.

When my career began to take off with the Purefoods Chunkee Giants, I felt a sense of success, as anyone would, but I also felt a strong sense of bitter vindication. I was getting back at all those people who caused me to feel ashamed of myself. I had risen up through the ranks and was in the running to be one of the top performers in one of Asia's best leagues and, while all that may sound great, it's a not a complete life and it didn't make me a complete person. Had I not been injured, paralyzed, and permanently sidelined, I might have gone on that way forever, letting basketball be my identity, never forcing myself to discover how much more I was and how much more I could give.

***

Extravagant triumphs and crushing defeats are often two sides of the same coin. The wisest among us know it is better not to get too down when misfortune befalls us and not to get too high when good things come our way. The reason is simple: life is about maintaining balance. I'm not talking about the balance that comes from avoiding too much alcohol or unhealthy food. I'm talking about the kind of balance that comes from being centered in one's own identity. This was the balance I was missing in my life.

Always a people-pleaser, I endured taunting and mean jokes from coaches, trainers, and my teammates because I wanted to be liked. I didn't want to anger them by speaking up and defending my dignity as a person. Had I been centered enough in my own identity and sense of self, I would have seen that being liked, being easy going, being a team player, didn't mean I had to let myself be abused. There is a balance between being tolerant and being a doormat.

This kind of balance has been referred to as "the Tao" or "the Way of the Middle" and I believe that one ignores it at their peril. Today people often overlook the Way of the Middle as a true path to happiness and satisfaction and allow themselves to bounce from one extreme to another. Our world is full of extreme politics, extreme obsessions, and extreme habits. Following the Way of the Middle means not overreacting to every little thing or focusing our energies on either side of an issue to an extreme degree. It means seeing all the shades of gray in a world that is becoming more stridently black and white. While my personal belief system, Christianity, doesn't speak of this concept overtly, following this way means to live as Jesus himself lived, not caring about people's opinions and remaining true to ourselves and what we know is right even if it is not popular.

In the New Testament, we often see Jesus going against the mainstream and we see that He was criticized for hanging out with the wrong crowd. The book of Mark tells the story of the Messiah being questioned by religious authorities for "eating with sinners." Jesus famously retorted, "It is not the healthy who need a doctor, but the sick."

One of the reasons I chose to be a follower of Jesus is that His life reflects this commitment to being even-keeled and free-thinking. In the face of overwhelming pressure to toe the line from the Pharisees and religious experts of the day, Jesus knew His purpose and He would not depart from what He was called to do and He explained this to his critics with respect but without compromise. I guess you could say He was tremendously balanced.

I often imagine that Jesus, if He were living in a time such as today, would not have hired a PR firm to help "control the narrative." Neither would He have felt the need to use social media to guide the story so that His Q-rating would increase. Jesus was a man who knew that His path would ultimately lead Him to be crucified at the hands of the Roman—the ultimate thumbs down, if you will--but He still went out and lived life to the fullest.

Now I know many of you who are reading this may not be Christians and I respect that. I am, in fact, going to tackle a lot of concepts in this book that are not exclusively Christian in nature. Learning to be even-keeled and to live a balanced life full of gratitude, freeing yourself from harmful expectation and burdens of popular opinion, were all ideals that were expressed by spiritual greats such as Lao Tzu and Gautama Buddha and they are, I feel, universal truths.

Across all faiths and culture, spiritual leaders have declared time and again that success, as we have defined it in this world, is an illusion. Success is not the accumulation of millions of dollars in our bank accounts. It is not the acquisition of multiple beach properties that appreciate over the years. All these things can be taken from us in an instant. Success is about knowing who we are and being so unshakably centered in our identity and purpose that nothing can take us off the path that we are meant to take in life.

***

The words of Jack Whittaker echo in my mind: "I don't like what I've become." They resonate with me because I have experienced the opposite: my paralysis forced me to become the person I love today. Before, I was living life as a lottery winner might, spending money that came too easily, caring too much about what other people thought of me, and always trying to impress the who's who of the Manila in-crowd.

I was on a dangerous path but, as it is for so many of us, the dangers only became evident when something remarkable happened. I say remarkable, not tragic, because that was what my paralysis was. In both good and bad times, extremes rear their ugly heads. As seen in that article in *Time* magazine, the worst the world had to offer presented itself just when those lottery winners thought they were being given a chance to discover the best. The coin spins and good turns to bad. I thought I had been dealt the worst blow possible but then the coin landed and I discovered blessings I couldn't have imagined before my injury.

Maybe there was a time in your life when you were overly upset about something. Perhaps you were passed over for a promotion. Maybe you didn't get that house you wanted or get into the school of your dreams. Maybe your life goals were derailed because someone in your family got sick. These losses and setbacks can make you feel defeated but it is important to consider that maybe these disappointments were designed to set you down a different path and will be responsible for most of your joy in the future. My paralysis helped me uncover the person I was meant to be. Just like my Lord and Savior, I now know my purpose and calling in life and that is only because of my "unfortunate" accident.

Don't get me wrong, being paralyzed is not an easy thing to deal with. I barely sleep for more than an hour straight each night because the spasms in my back are so painful that they wake me up regularly. Standing again for the first time took a herculean effort on my part and the dedication of an army of trainers and physical therapists who believed in me. I worked harder than I ever had as a professional athlete just to be able to take a few steps with these broken limbs of mine. But do you know what? Every bit of the experience has been worth it because I am now who I was always meant to be.

I would like to submit to you these three takeaways to consider as this chapter comes to an end:

1.) **Whatever happens in this life, there are two sides: one good and one bad.** One event will always have a negative force and positive force attached to it. It is your job to manage these forces in order to "stay in the middle" and be true to yourself while we experience the variety of life's episodes.

2.) **Only when you *decide* to be happy will you actually experience true happiness.** If I can be happy after being paralyzed and confined to a wheelchair, there is no limit to what you can do when you make the *decision* to be happy.

3.) **Being even-keeled brings out the best in you.** It allows you to be self-aware and this awareness allows you to be present in the moment. This is the ultimate state of happiness: to fully enjoy what is in front of you right now in spite of any external circumstance.

As the most prestigious athletic trainers in the world say, "strength is nothing without stability."

CHAPTER 2
"THE PERILS OF FAME"

When the ambulance finally arrived at the Ynares Center in Antipolo, I had been lying on the floor of the court for a full ``40 minutes. For some reason, the ambulance that was normally stationed near the stadium in case of emergencies had been sent away early. Eventually, it returned and rolled away from the curb outside the stadium *en route* to the hospital with me, the team doctor, and my girlfriend inside. It was, I recall, the roughest ride of my life. If you are not familiar with the topography of Antipolo, it is basically a city built on a series of hills. Subsequently, my ambulance ride was a rocky, zigzagging journey that began at the top of a hill and descended steeply and haphazardly towards the low plains where Makati, the central business district of Manila, lay.

The day had seen storms and inclement weather and traffic conditions, never ideal to begin with, were not at their finest. The ambulance driver was aware of the time that had elapsed since my injury occurred and wanted to get to Makati Medical Center as fast as he could but the situation on the road meant that moving even a few kilometers presented a monumental challenge. The driver performed evasive maneuver after evasive maneuver, fighting through the congestion. A few feet behind him I was fighting my own battle to stay alive.

The jerky movement of the emergency vehicle had triggered a feeling of motion sickness. I began to throw up. The problem was that, because I was paralyzed, I couldn't swallow my own vomit and this created a choking hazard. I was drowning. I tried to force myself cough. If I couldn't get enough air into my lungs, I would suffocate before we even reached the hospital.

As the ambulance weaved its way around the sharp turns in the road, I was faced with a decision. I could wave the white flag and give in to death which hovered above me like a specter. No one would think any less of me. No one would know that I had let go. I thought about how horrible my life would be as a quadriplegic and I was tempted to give up my struggle and end it right then and there.

Then I thought about my family. I thought about my sister, Dana, who had graduated from college that very same day in the US. I thought about my brother, James, who needed me to be there for him. I thought about my parents and how it would break their hearts to lose a son. And so, I fought. I fought for my life with everything I had. Using every ounce of strength I could muster, I forced myself to cough out my own vomit and eject it from my system. I was scared, confused, and unsure what the future held for me but, at that moment, I knew at the very least I was going to live.

***

In the first few years of my career, frustrated by ribbing from my teammates and discouraged by the constant benching I received from one of the country's best coaches, I began to create an off-court reputation for myself as a hard partier. If I couldn't be the star player, I could at least be the life of the party. I drank and reveled until the wee hours of the morning, a habit which I took with me when I transferred to a new team despite the fact that it had begun to affect my ability to contribute as a player.

Manila in those days was paradise for hedonists like me. Its central business district, Makati, was home to more than 100 nightclubs, each with its own unique appeal and rich with possibility for a casual hook-up or two. My friends and I would regularly begin our bar-hopping around 11 pm. We met at the classic Porch bar and ordered our usual shots of *Boy Bastos* which translates to Rude Boys. It's a cocktail designed to get you drunk before the night even starts. With our inhibitions properly loosened, we would then head to four or five additional establishments. We would blow our paychecks on round upon round of drinks, invite a few women to join us if we felt like it, and continue on like this until three or four in the morning.

That particular time in my life presented a perfect setting to explore the meaning of the word *vice*. Though, as it turns out, the most irresistible vice for me in Manila was not the ubiquitous bars or nightclubs. It was not the rampant recreational drugs that were passed around from one wealthy socialite to another. The vice that called out to me the loudest, my kryptonite as it were, was the fame itself. It played directly into that far too often unrequited desire of mine to be seen and heard, to be glorified and lauded. My excessive partying kept me front and center in Manila's social circles and my lack of moderation brought me as much renown and notoriety as my skills on the court.

***

Many books have been written about the power and strength of habit. Charles Duhigg, author of the bestselling book *The Power of Habit*[2], and James Clear, author of the equally successful *Atomic Habits*[3], both write about why habits stick with us. They suggest that there are four phases to a habit: the Cue, the Craving, the Response, and the Reward. The Cue is the phase where the brain interprets a signal and causes a person to move towards something. In Manila, the Cue for me could be as simple as the neon lights flickering to signal the opening of a bar or the sound of clinking shot glasses as people raised a toast to their seeming immortality. These sights and sounds were the trigger to step into my Life of the Party persona, a role that had become almost an official title for me.

Authors such as Duhigg and Clear note that without those four phases, the Cue, the Craving, the Response, and the Reward, a habit fails to stick with us. If even one piece of that puzzle is missing the habit won't form; it won't solidify into a lifelong behavior. Unfortunately, all the pieces fell into place for me. My bad habit of drinking and partying most nights was cued by the sights and sounds of Manila's nightlife and fueled by a desperate craving to be admired. I responded by continually seeking out parties and events to attend where I was rewarded with attention and acclaim. I was

---

[2] Charles Duhigg, *The Power of Habit* (Random House, 2012).
[3] James Clear, *Atomic Habits: An Easy & Proven Way to Build Good Habits & Break Bad Ones* (Penguin, 2018).

king in this realm, MVP of the party scene. What did it matter if it was affecting my ability to perform at my day job?

Like most people with a bad habit to hide, I became pretty adept at covering up my social misadventures. On game days, I was present and made an acceptable show of wanting to play. I put on my uniform and warmed up. I even went as far as fake-taping my ankles. In professional basketball, ankles are considered the most common location for injuries and most players will tape theirs in order to help prevent sprains. I would tape the top part of my ankles and shins, just enough that it showed above my socks and shoes, but I never bothered with the lower part of my ankle because I knew I was going to find a way to stay off the court. I made a good enough presentation of wanting to play that I could almost fool even myself. Then, when the coach decided to bench me, I was able to play the victim: it was my coach's issue, not mine, I would think. He was selling me short and not giving me a chance to shine.

I had resigned myself to a fatalistic, self-defeating mentally: no matter how well I did at practice, I was not going to break through and get the minutes that I deserved. This gave me the justification I needed to feel better about going out at night and getting wasted instead of working on the various facets of my game that needed improvement. This, in turn, resulted in more benching. It was a vicious circle and through it all, I would ask myself what was the point of it all if the coach was never going to see my potential anyway. I might as well enjoy myself and find recognition where I could.

***

The year 2000 marked the turn of the millennium, a numerical milestone for society, and the year when the world's first reality show, "Survivor," premiered on CBS to a global audience. Sixteen strangers were placed on an island for thirty-nine days, provided with meager rations and no shelter, and pitted against one another in various challenges. Viewers were glued to their sets to see who would be the last man or woman standing and a new social phenomenon was born: he who attracts the most attention wins regardless of strength, intelligence, or moral fiber.

The cultural repercussions of this global phenomenon were felt years later when Facebook and YouTube made their respective debuts. YouTube, in particular, had a business model for video content makers in which the amount of money paid to them corresponded to the amount of views a particular video received, regardless of quality. Like contestants on a deserted island competing to be the final Survivor, success for these content makers did not rely on talent, skill, or even luck it seemed. As long as you could get enough people to watch your video, whether they loved it or hated, you had it made.

This helped create the current cultural climate in which we find ourselves participating in a twisted sort of anti-meritocracy where what you put into the world matters less than how successfully you are able to promote it. You don't even need a product to sell if you can sell yourself. Talent and hard work fall to the wayside in favor of luck and the ability to self-promote. Our current generation believes that you can say or do anything and even make money at it as long as you have 5 million followers on YouTube.

Now before anyone dismisses me as an out-of-touch old man bashing the younger generation, I will point out that I speak from experience. Lurking behind the very unhealthy lifestyle I was living in Manila was the desire for the same kind of attention that social media professionals aspire to—fame for the sake of fame. Had YouTube come along a few years earlier, I probably would have been putting out meaningless or even destructive content solely to get likes or followers.

Morality has become subjective with people looking to their followers rather than within for guidance. They don't ask themselves *Is this right? Should I do this?* They post it and if it gets enough hits and their followers increase then it must be okay and they continue to post similar content. In December 2017, a social media superstar was criticized for posting a video shot in Japan's *Aokigahara Forest*, also known as the Suicide Forest. In the video, the social media star encountered a body and showed it in full while making jokes in the background. The video was taking down but not before 6.5 million people had viewed it. The public was suitably outraged by this man's actions but many of his followers still defended him.

While the video shot in Japan might have been his most extreme, many of his videos were full of similar types of shock and awe and his behavior consistently showed little regard for the culture of any country he visited. And yet, before the controversy, this YouTube superstar was estimated to earn approximately $12.5 million a year, making him the 4th highest paid YouTube video uploader in the world. His rudeness and boorish behavior resulted in more views, clicks, and followers which then encouraged him to make more of the same types of incendiary videos.

This is the way it was for me when I was living it up in Manila. I had a reputation and was known. It didn't matter what I was known for as long as people were watching me and if I noticed that a particularly outrageous action garnered the most attention then I was sure to follow that up with something even more insane. What I was putting out there didn't matter, what was important was that people were watching.

Imagine that Hollywood only had around ten actors and actresses who were relevant. These ten people got all the best roles, the most media coverage, and the biggest paychecks. Now imagine that in order to maintain that relevance, each of those actors and actresses had to continually do things that were increasingly rude, audacious, or outlandish in order to one-up each other. They would basically function like wrestlers on Vince McMahon's WWE, acting out convoluted scripts which are played out as real life and sold to the public as reality. In Manila, that was the dystopian world I was a part of. I hadn't yet reached the elite level of the ten or so celebrities who mattered most but I was certainly trying my hardest to get there.

By 2006, the quest for fame had begun to consume most of my time and energy and it wasn't until I was out of a job, dropped by the Alaska Aces, that I began to take basketball seriously again. The very thing that was supposed to set me apart and bring me fame and admiration had taken a back seat to the celebrity status my social carousing had brought me. But the predicament of being a free agent with no prospects of a team and the subsequent fallout of the accident that caused my paralysis helped me realize that fame without substance was a vain conceit.

Over all, I don't have an issue with social media and I respect people who can use that type of platform to share their talent and message with the world. Nor do I have an issue with people working hard to achieve financial success. I have great respect for people like Warren Buffet who has earned billions of dollars using his extraordinary talent for investing. And I love hearing about it when a deserving songwriter who may have been overlooked by the music industry is able to build an online fan base for their music and make their dreams of superstardom come true. That's because I firmly believe in the importance of pursuing a skill or talent over fame.

If I had been wiser, I would have put all my energy into building my skills as a professional athlete rather than trying to hit every bar in Manila on working weeknights. A person who attracts a significant amount of attention is not necessarily someone who deserves it and I found this out the hard way. The advent of social media has created a world in which fame is prized but lacks meaning. At the risk of sounding older than my actual age and inspiring an "okay, Boomer" response, I believe it becomes a real problem when fame is pursued without any regard for purpose and social media influencers are rewarded for self-indulgent antics that contribute little if anything to society.

My past experience has given me the courage and awareness to speak out against this movement. For the longest time, I pursued fame without understanding why I wanted it and without any real sense of how I wished to achieve it. When I had it within my grasp, I found that it did not deliver the satisfaction I thought it would. Fame, in and of itself, is an empty promise and to continually promote this emptiness to a younger generation will only bring folly. Our children will lose sight of what it truly means to chase a dream and be successful if all they are taught is to seek is the approval of others through likes, comments, and a growing list of followers.

There are a few critical points that I have learned in examining my quest for fame in light of my paralysis and I'll start with the most important:

1.) **The people who will follow you when you pursue fame as a primary purpose in life will be the first ones to leave you during any form of turbulence.** Consider the growing trend of "Cancel Culture." When people only like you because other people seem to like you, your downfall will be swift. I learned this the hard way when people stopped visiting me in the hospital.

    About 4 months into my ordeal I was still very much paralyzed. I had stopped being an inspiration to my teammates who had just won a championship and was becoming a liability in the eyes of management. Fans saw me as "old news" and were wondering about the new power forward who would take my place in the rotation. A few months after that, my girlfriend left me because she didn't want to be saddled with a man who couldn't move from the neck down and required constant care. I learned that she had left me for another man by watching one of the TV talk shows I had tried so hard to get onto back when I was playing. All the fame I had worked to build backfired in a profoundly cruel way.

2.) **Fame built without any consideration of legacy provides no quenching for the soul.** It is only proper that some people to get their due recall in history. Oskar Schindler, for example, was an industrialist who is credited with saving the lives of 1,200 Jews during the Holocaust. He deserves every bit of recall that history can bestow upon him. Frederick Banting received the Nobel Prize in medicine in 1923 along with John James Rickard Macleod. They discovered (or more technically, isolated) insulin and both deserve widespread fame and recognition for their efforts. To contrast the contributions of the three figures above with the contributions of a YouTube sensation such as the person we described earlier further demonstrates the difference between people whose fame means something and those whose fame is a hollow artifact. There has to be a deeper and more significant purpose in life than to be validated by the likes and re-tweets of a million strangers.

3.) **Fame represents a trade-off in the scariest sense of the word.** We often hear tales of how people sell their souls to the devil for a taste of fame or fortune. It's a reoccurring trope in literature and folk tales. Sadly, at one point during my journey as a paralytic, I would have readily made a deal with the devil. I would have traded my soul if he would have only given back to me what I had lost. Thinking about how desperate I was in those days still sends chills through my entire body.

Pursuing fame at the expense of one's morals and soul seems to be where this world is heading. We live in a society that does not care about the exploitation of others as long as we get to watch the train wreck. It's entertainment and it is why people feel emboldened to take extreme, cruel, and hateful stances on social media. They know that for every person they offend and alienate, they will find one or two more who can't wait to watch the fireworks explode. Millions of people justify moral bankruptcy by declaring "it's all in good fun," swapping their souls for entertainment. May we guard ourselves against such an unfair trade!

***

I have long believed that I went through what I did in order to warn people. While I did not achieve the heights of fame that some of you may attain one day, I did experience enough to know that most of it was sugar water--sweet but devoid of the nourishment my soul needed. I built up fame based on moments of shallow self-indulgence and, as quickly and easily as it had come, it was gone. Satisfaction was fleeting and the overall feeling left behind was one of emptiness.

The tantalizing promise of fame calls to mind the sirens of Greek mythology who attempted to lure Jason and the Argonauts onto the rocks where their boat would be dashed to pieces. These were the same sirens encountered by Odysseus in Homer's epic poem, *The Odyssey*. These myths tell us that the heroes, Jason and Odysseus, asked to be tied down in order to resist the lure of the poisonous siren songs. Today, we must be willing to take measures as extreme as those heroes did to fight the pull of easy or undeserved fame. To save ourselves from crashing into the shores of empty promises, we would do well to heed the warnings of those who have experienced existence in those bleak lands.

When I was on top of the world, feeling invincible and immortal, I seared my conscience through one bad decision after another. The habit loop--Cue, Craving, Response, and Reward—played endlessly and I wasted countless nights intoxicated, partying with the wrong crowd. Being cut down by my paralysis taught me that fame without virtue is a vain conceit and whoever devotes his life to such a cause does so at the peril of his inner identity and essence. The sirens of fame promised me a kingdom and so I allowed myself to drift off course only to discovered that my kingdom was nothing but a wasteland of emptiness and frustration.

I pray not only for my generation but for the generations after mine. I hope that we will all realize an important concept: fame without significance or purpose is a poisonous trap to be avoided at all costs. By contrast, having something important to offer the world and to become famous as a byproduct of that important offering is eternally more significant.

CHAPTER 3
"ABSOLUTE POWER"

After having survived the nearly hour-long ambulance ride from hades, I was wheeled into the emergency room at Makati Medical Center. I started looking for familiar faces and sure enough, there they were: Harvey Carey, Alex Compton, and Kalani Ferreria. These men, also Filipino-Americans from the PBA, had been three of my closest friends. A part of me was upset that they had actually gotten to the hospital before me but another part of me was just relieved to see them. I looked for other comforting faces in the crowd that had gathered at the hospital and there was one person I couldn't miss. This was Edward Joseph Feihl, EJ for short.

EJ had been a teammate in my first season as a professional with the Alaska Aces. The thing that made EJ stand out was that he was seven feet tall. I had never met a 7-foot tall Filipino before. He was a real giant, standing nearly a head taller than anyone else out there. EJ, however, was a gentle giant; his large frame housed a tender heart and an empathetic soul. When he saw me, he came to the side of my gurney and wept aloud. I appreciated EJ's tearful gesture and realized that he was weeping, not in sorrow for me, but in relief that I was still alive. His heartbreaking cry reminded me that what had happened could have been a lot worse.

That comfort was short-lived, however. I quickly became aware that I was more helpless than I had ever been in my life. I couldn't move anything from my neck down and I had trouble even breathing. It was at this moment that God chose to send some very special angels in human form to help me. One of them was my Aunt Ina, my dad's sister, who was supposed to fly home to the US a day after my accident but cancelled her trip back as soon as she heard what had happened to me.

Aunt Ina stayed with me until my parents were able to fly to the Philippines and she was a pillar of strength for me in those early days. A nurse back home, Ina was very familiar with medical procedures and her knowledge proved invaluable. She made sure that the hospital staff injected me with steroids when I needed them most and I later learned that, if she had not insisted I get the steroids when I did, my body would have built up too much scar tissue in my neck area and my recovery would not have been possible. To this day, I am grateful for my Aunt Ina's guidance and that she willingly dropped everything to make sure I was okay.

Being hurt in such a public manner—during a live, nationally-televised game--made me a pseudo-celebrity in the hospital. Several prominent people from the Philippines made it a point to visit me during my stay there. I was able to keep my spirits up and, at first, had some hope that the injury was not too bad. I kept praying that it was just a stinger, a compressed nerve that would come right again, allowing everything to get back to normal. I hung on to the dream that I would be able to don my playing jersey once again and make a comeback. Eventually, the doctors informed me that the X-Rays and CT scans had confirmed that it was a fracture of the C5 and C6 vertebrae. It was then that they told me that I had only a 4% chance of ever walking again.

The doctors said I would need to be placed in traction. They would put screws in my head and attach a halo and weights to decompress my vertebrae and pop them back in place. As I was experiencing traction, I heard actual popping. I had heard similar sounds when Mick fell on me, only this time, the noises brought relief. The traction treatment brought some sensation back to my feet for the first time since I was injured. I still couldn't move my toes but I could feel something. Even if the doctors were only giving me a 4% chance of walking, traction and the small improvements it brought gave me a glimmer of hope.

It was hard to remain positive and upbeat for long, however, when I was being faced with such powerlessness. I had never had to depend on so many people to do the most basic things for me. It hit me hardest when I realized that other people would have to clean me up after I soiled myself. I had gone from being one of the most sought-after athletes in the country to not even being able to go to the bathroom independently. I thought about my past desire for power and prestige and realized how much farther I was from obtaining that while lying on a motorized hospital bed.

***

Niccolo Machiavelli was an Italian politician and philosopher who wrote the quintessential text on power. In his infamous tract *The Prince*, written in 1513, Machiavelli makes a clear distinction between theology, politics, and moral philosophy. *The Prince* was, and still is in many ways, an influential roadmap outlining how already powerful rulers can become even more powerful and has inspired dictators and malevolent politicians for centuries.

One of Machiavelli's key insights involves the idea that morality is irrelevant in politics and that it is impossible to judge the use of power since power cannot be sorted neatly into boxes labeled Good and Bad. In order for a prince to maintain safety, security, and stability in his state, he must be able to behave in a completely reprehensible fashion if the need arises. While there is some debate regarding Machiavelli's true intent in writing these passages--to condemn the use of power or to praise it--what is clear is that hundreds of political leaders from Napoleon to Hitler and Mao Zedong were influenced by these writings and used them to justify abusing power.

Machiavelli commented on the effective application and maintenance of power by any means necessary as well as the consolidation of power, or storing up of power until massive influence is achieved. These ideas can clearly be seen in action today. Today, public opinion is bought and sold at digital farms where thousands of cellular phones are held at one location with a corresponding amounts of bots. These bots are basically fake accounts that leave comments and engage in trolling, presenting lines of argument not born of proper discourse but of bullying and shock tactics.

Political divisions are intensifying. Nations are tearing at themselves from within while people are reporting all time low levels of satisfaction with their lives and the direction their countries are heading. I believe the reason for this is that we have fallen prey to two very cunning and *Machiavellian* tricks played upon us by people in power, whether that is political power, religious power, or social power.

One of the oldest tricks people in power play is to convince others that the general consensus, i.e. the view with the most support, is the most morally correct stance. This is trick was played to perfection by a certain Joseph Goebbels, Nazi Minister of Propaganda in Hitler's Third Reich, but it is also a tactic of the school yard A-crowd--"Come on! Everyone is doing it." People of the modern world must be wary of the ideology of the majority as it is the most common way a politician or leader will maintain power and has been used to justify all manner of social ills over the centuries.

We tend to think of Peer Pressure being a problem of adolescence but more than ever it is following people into adulthood even if we no longer call it that. If we look at what is happening in our society today, we see that there is very little critical thought occurring in the debate rooms of social media and most users tend to live in social media bubbles filled with like-minded individuals. When one of our closest friends shares an article with a sensational headline and a large number of our other friends "like" it or share it on their own page, do we bother to check the sources or consider the other side of the argument? Rarely. Sometimes the headline is enough for us and we share it without even reading the article, getting a little buzz when we do because we know we are sending it out to people who think like us who will "like" it too.

On the flip side, we have an increase in personal attacks unleashed by professional trolls against Facebook users who express criticism of whoever or whatever is funding the trolls. These online attacks are acts of bullying, plain and simple, and carry more weight than they should because of the value we have placed on being in the general consensus. After such an attack, the bullied person will think twice about offering a differing view point on future posts and once again our exposure to new ways of thinking shrinks.

All this is to the politician or leader's gain. They have isolated us from anyone who disagrees with them and convinced us that these people are enemies, not only theirs but ours as well. We are now linked to this leader in a "we're in it together/on the same team" sort of way and critical thinking is lost because we have internalized the criticism and made it personal. We must ask ourselves how we can identify structures of power and become more aware of the ways in which we are being manipulating in order to protect ourselves. These type of tactics will only benefit the ruler, not the people he or she rules.

The second trick an unethical ruler or leader might use to manipulate people is the exchange of favors in order to gain unwavering loyalty. To maintain power, those in authority will often perform favors for others in order to get something that they need. In politics this is often called Pay for Play. An example would be a politician offering to loosen regulations or grease the wheels for new business ventures outside of the country to benefit a wealthy businessman who then promises to donate generously to the politician's super PAC.

In the Philippines, I noticed that roads were generally constructed and repaired just before election season. The roads may have been badly in need of repair for years but the funds to fix the roads were made available just before it was time to vote so that the service the politician had provided to their electorate would be fresh in voter's minds when the polls opened. A prime example of this occurred in 2013 when Typhoon Haiyan hit the city of Tacloban in the Philippines. Millions of people reached out to help including a politician up for reelection who handed out relief bags with his face plastered all over them. Were the supplies in the bag much needed? Yes. But the assistance felt like a campaign stunt and it struck at the dignity of the citizens whose lives had been disrupted and who were now being used for political gain.

So why does this matter you ask. Well, being paralyzed fourteen years ago gave me a fresh perspective on power. I went from being someone who had some semblance of power and who wanted more, to being a person who was literally and figuratively powerless. I couldn't even change the channels of the hospital TV because I could not move anything below my neck. I struggled to regain control of my body but I felt a weight lift as I learned to let go of the need for the other sorts of power and influence that I had been clutching at so desperately. Lord John Dalberg Acton, a British historian, famously said "Power tends to corrupt. Absolute power corrupts absolutely." When I freed myself from the pursuit of power, I freed myself from the pursuit of corruption and that felt good.

In all my desperate wrangling for power, I never reached the level of evil that people like Goebbels or Hitler did, but I was guilty of participating in this process of trying to consolidate and maintain power to the detriment of those around me. As I mentioned before, I was only really nice to people who could do something for me. In Manila, where social status is often flaunted, there were people I considered beneath me and I did not treat them with the respect they deserved because their ability to affect my future in any positive way was limited. This is something that I have deep remorse for in my heart. I let power corrupt me and my view of friendship and how I should treat my fellow human beings.

* * *

The world is much different for me now. Living in Arkansas years after the accident, I have made a complete 180. I am no longer the person trying to make it onto the VIP list in the hottest nightclub. I no longer care if my friends are powerful or if they have the right social connections. I wait my turn in line and I'd rather do a favor for someone than ask them for one in return.

Much of my healing has had to do with reading about how a few people in the past have subverted the traditional Machiavellian power structure and turned it upside down. It says in one of my favorite Bible verses: *"The kings of the Gentiles exercise lordship over them and those in authority over them are called benefactors. But not so with you. Rather, let the greatest among you become as the youngest, and the leader as one who serves[4]."*

These are the words of Jesus, a man who was more powerful than anyone who ever lived. Yet he chose to wash his disciples' feet and humbled himself in ways no other leader would ever consider. The more I reflect on this, the more I realize that the most effective way to subvert traditional power structures is to simply be willing to serve others.

When I could not do anything for myself, in my darkest days, there were people who literally cleaned my filth off of me. I am always thankful for those people and the care they invested in me and my wellbeing. While they may have been inconvenienced during that time, I hope that they received some unique satisfaction in knowing how greatly their actions blessed me and how their example helped me find joy in humility.

---

[4] Luke 22: 25-26 *The Holy Bible: New International Version, NIV* (Biblica Inc. 1973, 1978, 1984, 2011).

There was a time while I was still blind to my failings and the true path to happiness, a time when I wanted people to worship me. I wanted them to bow down before me—the best basketball player in the Philippines. I wanted to lord my successes over them and use their admiration to control them and empower myself in unhealthy ways. Now I am free of that desire for power and have experienced the kind of liberation that comes with knowing how insignificant I really am: I am just one of several billion people walking the planet. There is freedom in that. I don't have to try to control things all the time. I don't have to be overly angry all the time. I can accept that I don't control the actions of other people or how they react and respond to me and that no one owes me anything. I have learned that when you're too full of yourself, there is no room left inside for joy.

I don't crave adulation and authority anymore. I went from being a 6'4" tall athlete to a paralytic in a wheel chair. I was diminished in size and physical authority, something that had been a point of pride for me, but I learned that I didn't need the status and power that came with size or physical strength. What I needed was to emulate someone who deserved all the power in the world but craved none, a man who chose to be a servant in spite of his unlimited and total power. Although I know some of you will not agree with this as it is not in line with your personal faith, it is my belief that Jesus was the Son of the Lord Almighty. He could've done anything He wanted to those who tortured Him and hung Him on a cross to die. Instead He continued to think of others even up to the last minute of His earthly life.

I aspire to be like that man: the servant leader. I want to inspire others with truth and the light that outshines the darkness. Where people like Hitler, Stalin, and Pol Pot may have thought about subjugating entire populations, the only person I need to subjugate is myself. I need to master my desires and keep them in line with my purpose on this planet. My injuries and the subsequent revelations it brought have liberated me from the mindless rat race and quest for power.

There is more to life than having followers. I know that we sometimes fantasize about being the dictator of our own small country or at least having the power to shape the society and world around us to our own ideals. There is a reason that a fair number of our most beloved fairy tales end with the hero or heroine ascending to a palace. It is not enough to have found love or escaped a life-threatening situation; we crave power to ensure that our new found happiness, our happy ending as it were, can't be taken from us. Of course, there is not enough power in the world to protect ourselves from everything.

We have to let go and accept that sometimes we will be hurt, physically and emotionally. We can't control other people but when we stop trying to gain power over them and over every little aspect of our lives, we can experience great freedom. I was paralyzed, lying on a lonely hospital bed, unable to move. My body had become a prison. I had lost my power to control people around me. I couldn't make them come to see me. I couldn't make them remain by my side. I had lost all outward power but through my experiences, I learned more about the power I had within. I didn't have to control everyone and everything around me. All I had to do was control my reaction and response to those things and the experience was mine to shape.

The next time you don't get your way in a situation, just walk away. Process what happened from a position of inner strength. You alone are the one who controls your actions. Don't be afraid that apologizing to someone will diminish you. Trust in your power to withstand the worst that anyone else can do and you will have attained freedom. Embrace power only as you use it to serve others and you will have no need to control them. They cannot take from you what you give to them freely. This is the kind of liberation that my paralysis has taught me: there is infinite delight in being humble. We don't have to be the most important person on earth at all times. We just have to be the one that is important in meeting the needs of other people.

CHAPTER 4

"MULTIPLE MASKS PART I"

Listening to experts tell me that I would probably not walk again was, to say the least, not easy. On my second day in the hospital I was still adjusting to my new reality but I was relieved to know that my parents had made plans to fly to the Philippines and I was looking forward to the day that I would see my Dad as he was scheduled to arrive first.

I was on a real roller coaster during those early days. At some moments, I was filled with a fire and desire to prove to the doctors that their opinions didn't matter. After all, I'd played my way onto the Purefoods' roster despite the odds and all the naysaying. But during other moments, I would fall into a wallowing self-pity, questioning why I had to go through this entire ordeal and wondering if I even cared to go on. Although I was able to feel some sensation in my legs following traction, I still couldn't move them. I kept thinking about the big contract I would surely miss out on and I felt like it was a cruel prank: I came to Manila in 2003 looking to make it big in the professional leagues and, just when that goal was within my reach and I was about to carve out a name for myself, this happened.

I put on a brave face and hid the darkness that was growing in my mind, something I was accustomed to. I had become quite adept at wearing masks throughout my life. I often hid what I truly felt in order to please other people. I couldn't stand conflict of any kind and so I let other people say whatever they wanted to say in front of me. I may have been seething or hurting on the inside but I had such a great poker face that no one would ever have known. The problem was, because I was so used to wearing these masks, I had reached adulthood struggling to recognize what the real me looked like.

* * *

In the first century B.C.E., actors in Greek theater commonly wore large masks to mark the character they were playing on stage and to this day we still use the comedy and tragedy masks as a symbol of the theater. Other elements of these early theater traditions have survived as well. For instance, the Greek word for actor, *hypokrites*, has made it into common use in the English vocabulary as "hypocrite." There are two theories on what the Greek word actually means. Some say it comes from the word *hypokrisis* which means "jealous" or "acting out." Others believe the meaning comes from splitting the word in two: *hypo*, meaning "under," and *krisis*, coming from *krinein* and meaning "to decide." Essentially, put together, the word would translate to "a decision from below" or sometimes, "an interpreter from below."

This latter breakdown is where we get the English concept of the word hypocrite and I like the concept that a hypocrite is an "interpreter from below." This implies something hidden or lying beneath the surface, the man beneath the mask as it were. I feel it fits as a description for people who are not true to themselves or are hiding their true self behind a façade. This resonates with me because for many years I wore masks to hide who I was and hid behind a façade trying to be who I thought the world wanted me to be. I believe my inability to show my true image played a part in my injury and it certainly got worse for a time right after I was paralyzed. Some of the masks I wore before and after that fateful accident are as follows:

Mask 1: The Joker

This was the mask I wore when I played along as if I was part of the joke, laughing it up to hide my pain. During my first few practices with Alaska, my teammates gave me a lot of grief for being different. I was an American for starters. I had grown up in the US even if I was 100% Filipino by birth and I had a different way of moving. There was understated animosity because local talent felt that too many jobs in the PBA were being taken by Fil-Americans or Fil-foreign players. One of the most vocal critics against this was a Filipino legend named Jojo Lastimosa who happened to be an assistant coach with Alaska during my stint on the team. Jojo was a dynamic two guard whose clutch performances made him a natural crowd darling. He started the verbal jabbing by telling me that I looked like the guy from the movie *American Pie*.

The clowning went on for a long time. It started with the *American Pie* reference which seemed harmless enough but it took a darker turn. Throughout my life I had struggled with Attention Deficit Hyperactivity Disorder and dyslexia. I was diagnosed with both at an early age and found it very difficult to focus for prolonged periods of time and struggled with reading. It affected my grades in school and made reading a challenge. I had to focus so hard on each word to properly make them out that I often missed the meanings behind those words. Reading a short story was challenging and reading a complete novel was torture. The condition still affects me today and it takes me nearly three times longer than the average person to comprehend a passage in a book or magazine because I have to read it through multiple times before I fully understand what it says.

On the Alaska Aces, I was playing for a very intellectual coach who demanded that we know the Triangle Offense inside out. The Triangle Offense, made famous by Tex Winter and Phil Jackson of the Chicago Bulls, is not the type of offense that comes naturally to an ADHD sufferer such as yours truly. I knew that Dennis Rodman had mastered it so there was hope for me but there were so many cuts and variations to memorize that I struggled. As a result, my teammates gave me the unfortunate moniker of Eugene "What Happened?" Tejada. They laughed at me but I continued to wear the Joker Mask and joined them even though I was hurting inside.

I wore the Joker Mask during one of the most embarrassing incidents in my time with that team. We had just won a championship and the celebratory tradition was to call up players to receive their championship rings according to their skills and save the best or most valuable players for last. Being a benchwarmer, I expected that I would have been one of the first to get called up. I was okay with that. I knew that I didn't play much and I wasn't going to fool myself into thinking that I was considered valuable by this team. As they went down the roster, however, I noticed that my name hadn't been called. I started to feel good because I thought maybe, despite all their teasing, they might have considered me better than the other benchwarmers. However, the roll call progressed and they were finished with the benchwarmers and had begun calling out the star players. Something wasn't right. I knew that I was not considered better than John Arigo, even if I liked to think that I was.

And then it was over. All the names of my teammates had been read and the Master of Ceremonies proceeded to bid everyone good night. My name had never been called. I didn't know how to react. I was frozen in my seat, too hurt to say anything. I felt like I had been punched. The team waited for a couple of minutes before breaking out into collective laughter: "We're just kidding, Eugene! Here's your ring!"

I was devastated. Being called "Filipino Jason Biggs" is one thing but not being acknowledged in a ring ceremony was another. The joke had gone too far and what hurt the most was that it had been the idea of the team owner, Wilfred Steven Uytengsu, himself. I had really looked up to this man. Of course, I responded by donning my Joker Mask, the one with the biggest smile, and pretending to laugh alongside them.

I often asked myself why I let my teammates bully me this way. I'm sure many victims of bullying ask themselves the same thing. Why didn't I say something? Why didn't I do something? Maybe one quick punch to the nose would have shown that I wasn't going to take it and would have nipped it in the bud.

I am not judging my teammates or the team owner. What they did was wrong but I'll let them make peace with their actions. I am going to address my own failure to speak up. I should have trusted them enough to tell them the truth and give them the opportunity to show that they were better than that. The bottom line is, I was trying to please people more than I was trying to serve them. These things are not the same.

When we try to please people rather than serve them, we do not reveal our true character; we only reflect the other person's character back at them. Instead of letting my personality and my real heart shine through, I mirrored my teammates' mocking actions and laughed at myself in a way that was not genuine. Standing up to them would have been uncomfortable but it would have shown them an alternative way to view me. Instead of accepting the role of the team's clownish punching bag, I should have taken off my mask and allowed them to see the hurt they caused me, helping them understand the gravity of their actions while offering them forgiveness for any emotional injury they caused.

Mask 2: The Athlete

Jocks rule; Nerds drool! That was the message I learned as a kid. I grew up with a macho father who I never saw cry, not even when it would have been highly appropriate, like when a close relative passed away. Athletes are modern-day gladiators. We no longer watch barbaric killings in a coliseum but we let athletes battle against each other to show us what they can do and the link is still there. A number of our stadiums are still called coliseums for this reason. The arena I played most of my PBA games in was called The Araneta Coliseum which was, incidentally, the site of the famous bout between Muhammad Ali and Joe Frazier dubbed "the Thrilla in Manila."

Sports sometimes feel like they are a remnant from the days when men had to prove themselves physically in a rite of passage to claim their manhood and I had the idea that, if I didn't play well, I would somehow be less than a man. This added to my stress when I was warming the bench for Alaska: I was not proving myself. I was failing, not just as a player, but as a male. The benching became personal and painful. I never saw it for what it truly was: a challenge for me to improve my skills and my understanding of the game. I just thought that I was less of a man because I didn't play.

I wore the Athlete Mask for many years because I didn't want to be measured in any other way. I became upset when I didn't play well, even in high school, because it meant that I wasn't man enough for my father. This view really affected my relationship with him. It was an unyielding paradox: I wanted him to love me for who I was yet I always tried to gain his love through basketball. I played like a maniac because my entire identity was based on wearing the Athlete's Mask.

The downside was that I placed an unhealthy amount of weight on my success as an athlete. As long as our team was winning and I was playing well, I was ecstatic and the mask remained firmly in place. When I struggled with my performance, I became difficult and angry. I lashed out and resented everyone during these times because the mask began to slide and, if it slid too far, I might have to face what or who was underneath.

It is truly a tragedy that we often let sports define who we are. In the past this was predominantly a male issue but in our era of growing equality it is beginning to affect woman and girls as well. We put a premium on athletic ability and parents hope it will be their child's ticket to a good education and a better life. In an age where ESPN is a 24/7 network, we must remember that, while sports highlight positive things about athleticism and even, perhaps, the human condition at its finest and most raw, the athlete's performance on the court or field has very little to do with their character.

Athletes who have enjoyed great success on the field have messed up in life. Real winners off the pitch don't always have as much success in their athletic endeavors. All this gets lost in the hype though. What I learned is that wearing the Athlete Mask forces us into a kind of reductionist thinking: winning becomes the only thing that matters when we judge our athletes through these narrow lenses.

We should be wary of how this affects the way we view ourselves. The sooner we realize that sports do not define us, the better off we will all be. I have seen several former athletes fall into abject despair once they decided to "hang up their cleats for good." My retirement happened because of an unforeseen and tragic accident and, as a result, I struggled with it even more than an athlete who ends their career on their terms would. I remember lying motionless in the hospital bed, wondering, if I concentrated very hard, would I be able to move just enough to reach the pills beside my bed and consume them all at once. I wanted to end my life because sport had been taken from me and I was worth nothing. Or so I thought at the time although nothing could have been further from the truth! I gained so much once the paralysis had stripped away the masks and left me bare. I discovered that what was underneath was a more powerful version of me.

Mask 3: The Stoic

As Idina Menzel sang in the ubiquitous song "Let It Go"[5] from the movie *Frozen:* "Don't let them in, don't let them see / Be the good (boy) you always have to be."

---

[5] Anderson-Lopez, Kristen, and Robert Lopez. "Let It Go." *Frozen,* performed by Idina Menzel, Walt Disney Records, 2013.

Part of the reason my dad never cried was because of the Stoic Mask he wore. The Stoic Mask says that all men must be tough—they must not fall prey to weakness of mind as expressed in un-masculine emotion. I grew up in a culture where bravado and machismo were both celebrated and expected. Truth be told, I wanted my dad to cry when I saw him in the hospital after the accident. I believe there is a time for everything and a man shedding tears does not make him any less of a man. To be able to cry with my father for everything I had gone through, everything I had lost, would have been cathartic for me and probably for him as well. But, in the words of the great American poet and songwriter, Paul Simon: "A rock feels no pain / and an island never cries.[6]"

Unfortunately, those that wear the Stoic Mask want every man they meet to join their club. We circle back to that old majority rule concept here. If everyone agrees then it must be right. The cultural inhibitions and taboos placed on people that demand they suppress their natural emotional response has contributed to the destruction of families around the world. The divorce rate is at an all-time high with roughly half of all marriages in the US ending this way. Parents and children don't speak for years on end and lose the support and stability that extended family can offer as they move into new phases of their lives: retirement for the parents, and child-rearing years for the younger generation. This mask destroys relationships, platonic, familial, and romantic. In order for a healthy relationship to exist, a constant exchange and understanding of emotion must take place but this doesn't happen when we hide the feelings roiling inside us. We lock them away behind the Stoic Mask and suffer in silence and, eventually, we suffer alone.

Oh, what a tangled web we weave when we don those masks that hide our truth. And these are just three of the many masks we put on to deceive the people around us and ourselves. I will address a few more in the next chapter though it is important to note that sometimes we wear more than one mask at a time. It's all just layers to prevent people from seeing who we really are because we fear that, if they did, they might not like us. As I said earlier, somedays I felt so removed from myself that I couldn't even recognize my own face if I saw it in the mirror. And it's so easy to hide

---

[6] Simon, Paul. "I am a Rock." *The Paul Simon Songbook*. Performed by Paul Simon. CBS Records, 1965.

from one's self these days. We can project our insecurities onto other people through trolling on social media. We create elaborate masks and personas on Facebook and Instagram where life is a never-ending postcard-worthy vacation and all our flaws are filtered out.

The line between reality and fantasy has been blurred. We have stopped looking at people as human beings. Instead, we see only masks and we judge the actors who are in fact "hypocrites" in the truest sense of the word. One of my reasons for writing this book was to bring all of these diseases of the soul--the wearing of the masks, the pursuit of power etc.--out into the open. It is my hope that in time, we will begin to see that it is not worth it to wear the masks at all.

It takes a tremendous amount of energy to keep wearing these false faces day after day yet we get very upset when we are called out for wearing them. We "unfriend" people who speak truth to us like real friends should. Now, I am not an expert in psychology; what I share with you is from the experience I've gathered over the last fourteen years. I've been down this road and I've been the Joker, and the Athlete, and the Stoic. I wore these three masks to keep the world at a distance and might still be wearing them if I hadn't been paralyzed. Even today, if I'm not careful, I find myself slipping them on and I have to check myself but before I was not even aware that I was doing so. I was horribly blind to my hypocrite ways.

CHAPTER 5
"MULTIPLE MASKS PART II"

The third day at the hospital after the accident was probably one of the most difficult. The buzz around the freak accident had mostly died down and I had come to accept my fate. I knew that I was never going to play basketball professionally again and that I could forget about my upcoming contract.

While waiting for my immediate family members to arrive from the US, I continued to think about the many masks that were a hallmark of my life until a few days earlier. I knew that my situation had permanently changed and that the old masks would no longer fit. One by one they began to crumble and there were a lot of them. I never realized how many until I saw them in ruins. Picking up from the previous chapter they were as follows:

Mask 4: Mr. Invincible

You Only Live Once aka YOLO. It's one of the most uttered acronyms in the world today and is the sentiment behind The Mask of Invincibility. Invincibility is an illusion, of course. When we are at the top of our game, in the prime of our youth, we think that nothing can touch us. I am living proof that this sense of invincibility is nothing more than a falsity. The Mask of Invincibility makes people engage in risky behavior without a care for the consequences of their actions. At a poker table, no player is immune to a bad beat but, while most players may fold at all-in calls, others may take those calls and leave the player who went all-in with no chips at the end. That is essentially what happened to me in 2006.

Prior to the accident, I felt like I was on top of the world. I had bucked the odds and made it onto another pro team in Manila even after my release from Alaska, a team that had pretty much benched me for three years. I was dating a famous woman from Manila's upper echelon and got enough jealous looks from other men to know that I had achieved what I wanted on the romantic front. My plan was to play basketball for five to ten more years and then retire with a small fortune and return to my hometown of Hayward, California as a hero. I'd roll back into town rich, popular, and proudly displaying my "trophy wife" for all to see. I couldn't imagine a world where this plan could come undone. I couldn't fathom an outcome like the one that actually occurred.

The Mask of Invisibility I wore functioned as a blindfold and prevented me from seeing the ways in which I might be headed for a fall. I was taking recreational drugs and putting my body at risk with the way I partied at night. I thought I had everything I would ever need, everything I ever wanted. I was at the top of the food chain with good looks, health, a career that was taking off, and money at my disposal. Sure, there was this little matter of an expiring contract but, based on how I was playing, I figured that was a good thing. I could easily triple or quadruple the amount on that contract in the next few months.

I never did get a chance to negotiate a new salary. As I mentioned, when the paralysis happened, I instantly went from a prized asset to a major liability. Management cut me loose and they cut me quickly. I wasn't quite sure what I was going to do with my life after that. I had never even thought about a future without basketball--the Mask of Invincibility had ensured that I never bothered to come up with a Plan B. I was dealt a crushing hand. I went all-in and my bluff was called. That's how I felt lying in that dark hospital room without any movement below my neck.

Mask 5. The Material Guy

"It is not the man who has too little, but the man who craves more, who is poor." These are the profound words of Lucius Annaeus Seneca, a Roman philosopher and statesman who lived from about 4 BC to 65 AD.

He was allegedly associated with the Apostle Paul of Damascus and his writings on humanism were influential in his era and even through today.

Although my salary wasn't as high as that of an athlete playing in the American NBA, I was earning good money by most standards and I was proud of the amount I was being paid, putting great store in the prestige that this brought me. I enjoyed showing off my wealth and I felt validated among my peers. I never wanted to be seen as poor or in any way pitiable and, hey, doesn't society tell us that's what we should want: money, money, and more money? The Material Mask tells us that there is no clearer measure of a man's worth than the amount of money in his bank account. Wearing the Material Mask for many years made me miss out on developing friendships and relationships with at least several beautiful people who I did not consider to be important enough to associate with simply because they were not rich.

When I was paralyzed, I instantly went from well-to-do to charity case. I spent many years struggling with this because I refused to take off this mask even after my accident. When I first considered writing a book about my experiences, I did so with the thought that this might be my ticket back to financial success. At the time, I still felt entitled and I thought that the universe owed it to me to make me a millionaire, if not one way, then another. Because of the way things work in the Philippines, my medical expenses were not covered by the team or the league. I had signed a waiver saying that they were not liable for any bodily injury and so I still had a stack of hospital bills to pay. I figured that the universe granting me a best-selling book would even up the score a bit and settle the debts. All this did was sidetrack the project for eight years. I needed to find a reason beyond wanting to be rich again to propel my writing.

Constantly wanting more is an unavoidable consequence of the Material Mask. Since I was young, I was conditioned to believe that I needed to be the provider for my family. My skills on the basketball court were not just my ticket to a better life but a ticket to a better life for my family as well. Things really changed when I could no longer walk or even move my lower body. All hope I had that I would be able to provide for the people I loved was gone. Now I was more likely to become a burden than a savior and that idea was so devastating that it added to my suicidal thoughts. If I had no financial worth then what was the point of living?

Luckily, when we take off the Material Mask, we rid ourselves of the greed that accompanies it. We no longer have to base our identity on how much we have and we can begin to think of ourselves in more significant terms. In my case, one of the things that happened after I took off the Material Mask was that I began to understand who I was in Christ. I found out that I am unconditionally loved and that I no longer had to prove myself. God and his son Jesus Christ did not care what I had in my bank account. I was perfect the way He designed me to be and that would never change. At the time of my paralysis I had no idea how I might be able to earn money again but God provided and I found earning opportunities according to His perfect timing.

Mast 6: The Libertine

Hugh Hefner once said, "the major civilizing force in the world is not religion, it is sex." I hope I don't have to tell you that ol' Hef was wrong about that. Sex is not a civilizing force. It can turn people into animals and monsters very quickly. Religion is not necessarily a civilizing force either. It has led to wars and persecution throughout history the world over. I think Hef might have been starting down the right path but got sidetracked before he made it all the way to the correct conclusion: it is not sex or religion that civilizes the world but love. Sex and religion without love will do nothing but cause chaos and pain.

Most breakups are painful and it tends to add to the pain when you find out through a phone call that your incredibly hot actress girlfriend is cheating on you and then have that fact confirmed on a talk show while lying in a hospital bed unable to move. But part of what made my breakup so devastating was feeling the Libertine's Mask slide off my face. This was a role I could no longer play and the breakup just emphasized that. Wearing this mask meant that I was defined by my sexual conquests and once I was paralyzed, I couldn't fool myself that there were many of those left on my horizon.

There is tremendous pressure in the world today for males to measure themselves by the number of women they have slept with. This has led to abuses of power at the highest level. We not only condone using women in this way, we glorify it and reward the men who participate in this primitive power ritual--it is a power ritual and not a courtship ritual, make no mistake about it. Women have, for a large part of history, been unfairly objectified as an accessory to male achievement simply because a majority of the world's men wear the Libertine's Mask.

I had definitely bought into that toxic culture. I didn't realize that while the word Libertine implies freedom and refers to someone who is free and easy with members of the opposite sex--unrestrained and unfettered by morality--the Libertine's Mask had me in a kind of prison. As long as I held on to the belief that the most important thing about sex was that I was having a lot of it, I would be trading away pieces of myself for a few moments of physical satisfaction and pride.

When I reconnected with my future wife, Andrea, in 2012, I realized that I had to take off the Libertine's Mask once and for all. She was the first partner I'd had who demonstrated a profound sense of care for both my inner being and my mostly broken outer one. I began to think of love as putting the needs of another person ahead of my own, not just as making love in a sexual sense. I took those extra steps that Hugh Hefner had not been able to make and realized that to calm the storm inside and find civility and peace within, I needed to let myself love and be loved.

Andrea showed me that love is an act that is not focused on self. She showed me that it is different from mere lust. While everyone else may have seen me as a liability, she appreciated the person living inside the paralyzed body and she offered her unconditional support. She knew what she was getting into when we began dating but she never backed down. Her love is fierce and steadfast. I like to think that God validated her sacrifice and tremendous loyalty by blessing us with two wonderful twin boys. None of the things I enjoy today would have been possible without Andrea.

The Libertine Mask has imprisoned countless men and not all of them are lucky enough to find a woman like Andrea to free them from it. It is my hope that through this book, men will begin to realize the harm wearing this mask does to them and to the people around them. Lust has destroyed countless families and will destroy more unless the men who struggle with this issue find the courage to remove this mask. Additionally, measuring a man by his sexual prowess or conquests encourages risky behavior and diminishes the women in our society.

I remember feeling changed as this mask came off. When I made the decision to focus on love and not lust, I freed myself. I freed myself to be able to love my wife and provide her with the emotional connection she needs and make our marriage a successful one that grows more joyous every day. If I had continued wearing the Libertine's Mask, I would have never have truly recovered from my paralysis. I would have been a prisoner to the needs of my libido, judging myself to be a failure because I could not add enough notches to my belt indicating my conquests.

***

The Ideal Man as defined by society has to check a lot of boxes. He must be successful in everything he does, physically fit, strong, and free from defect or impairment. He has to demonstrate skill in fixing things and be good at sports, or at the very least be knowledgeable about them. He must be attractive to women but cool enough not to care what anyone thinks of him. He must not be emotional. He must never show fear or appear vulnerable. This is the Super-man image that society pushes on us through movies and marketing. We are bombarded with it. Women have their own list that they must adhere to as well and it is every bit as long as the list for men. These ideals only increase our insecurities and the feeling that we can never measure up. And so, we hide our flaws and our shortcomings and pretend to be more than we are when we were never not enough to begin with.

We don our masks but the more we rid ourselves of these masks--these lies--the more complete we will be as human beings. In the quest towards liberation, the first step is to come to terms with who we really are and declare that we will hide no longer. I have learned the following things in my quest:

1.) I didn't really have to be successful in everything I did. I actually learned the most from my failures. They made me stronger and they taught me to not judge other people when they go through their own "down cycles."

2.) Being whole has nothing do with the physical body and everything to do with the soul. I am more whole now than I had been prior to the accident.

3.) Since I can no longer collect rebounds and block shots for a living, I have focused on a more powerful inner kind of strength. This is the strength that allows me to be a great father to my two boys. It allows me to connect with my wife when she has had a trying day. It is this strength that allowed me to walk again when the experts thought it would be impossible. It is the strength that allows me to inspire people, even from my wheelchair.

4.) I am good at fixing some things but I realize that I can't fix everything. There are some fractures that won't heal. There are others that are going to take a lot more time. I've learned to trust the God of the Universe to do the fixing needed in my life.

5.) Sports are not everything. I used to be really good at sports. I was once a professional basketball player. I still *love* sports but in the long run, they are not really that important. They certainly are nothing to base a person's worth on but if they can bring us together as we cheer on our favorite team or inspire us to take better care of our bodies then they have a place in the world. That doesn't mean we should take them too seriously though.

When the Chicago Cubs won the World Series in 2016 after 110 years of title drought, I heard stories of people crying and declaring "I can die now." That level of passion is admirable but what if, instead of wasting it on a sports team, we approached life with our loved ones with that level of intensity? What if we were fierce fanatics in their lives, cheering their every accomplishment while staying by their side when they messed up, even if it took them 110 years to make it right again? If we could do that, the world and our homes would be profoundly better places.

6.) While not impossible, it is hard to get into bed with someone when you're a quadriplegic. The libertine lifestyle lost its appeal for me completely. I am truly satisfied with family life and the home that I share with Andrea and my boys. God created me to be a sexual being and I am completely comfortable exploring and fulfilling this sexuality within the context of my marriage to my beautiful wife.

7.) I do get emotional, especially when I remember all that I have gone through: the rigorous physical therapy sessions back in California where I darn-near killed myself just to be able to walk again, what it took to forgive Mick, the player who fell on my neck and inflicted the injury upon me, what it took to forgive my ex-girlfriend who left me. I get emotional when I look at my two boys. I consider them to be miracles of nature. I don't hold anything back when I get emotional thinking of the love that Andrea has showered upon me during these last six years of marriage. She has helped transform me into the man that I am today.

8.) I am still afraid of some things. I know that I can't control everything and, mostly, I am afraid that I'll lose the people I love. Then I remember that it is okay to be afraid, as long as my soul finds its rest in the Lord. In the Bible, the word *fear* is commonly used to mean respect or reverence. I have learned to turn fear of the unknown into *fear* for Him and to trust in God to work things out in my life.

9.) Being paralyzed has made me vulnerable in ways that I did not even think were possible and has led me to deeper encounters with God. It allowed me to open my heart to Him and to the people who were placed in my life for a reason.

I bring up these points to demonstrate that oftentimes, the best move is to step *away* from what society expects from us. Paralysis showed me that I would need to begin to grapple with my long-neglected issues of self. I had created masks and personas to hide the fact that I had no idea who I really was. I put these masks on and they are the reason it took me more than eight years to complete this book. Each draft I wrote prior to this one was written in a false voice from behind a mask. I wrote with the goal of projecting who I wanted people to think I was instead of who I really am. Those books were lies but I wasn't ready to be honest with myself; I said that the accident changed me, but I didn't say it changed me overnight! Just as rebuilding my broken body took time, rebuilding my sense of self was a work in progress as well.

It is my hope that, as you continue reading about my ongoing quest for a true state of liberation, you might consider identifying the masks you wear on an everyday basis and cast them off. Rebuild yourself in your truest image and leave behind the arbitrary list that society has created for us to follow. We are, after all, not actors lost in our own "hypocrisy." We are human beings who are free to be the very best we can be but only when we throw off the masks we hide behind.

CHAPTER 6
"DADDY'S BOY"

On the third day after my accident, a very welcome visitor walked through the door of my hospital room. My dad had finally made it to Manila after booking a flight as soon as he heard of my paralysis. I was expecting him to cry and hug me but he was stoic and appeared unmoved. There were no tears in his eyes and his face showed little emotion. Never the less, I was very glad that he was there. His arrival signaled a burgeoning of hope in my life especially since I was scheduled for surgery a few days after he got there. The procedure went as well as it could have gone and anticipation was building. After the surgery, a small crowd of supporters gathered around me and my dad to watch my reactions, looking for any sign of improvement.

Up to that point in time, seven days after the initial injury, I had not been able to move anything from the neck down. And then it happened—my right toe moved. I couldn't believe it. I kept asking the close friends and family around me, "Is it really moving?" People were crying and rejoicing with me. It was a big moment, bigger than any moment in any basketball game that I can remember. I looked for my dad and caught him out of the corner of my eye. For the first time in a long while, he looked like he was about to cry. He never let me see him in a completely emotional state, however. My dad, the first professional basketball player in our family and my tower of strength for so long, made a beeline for the bathroom. He held in his emotions until he got there because he didn't want his son to see his tears.

***

How can I try to explain?
When I do, he turns away again.
It's always been the same, same old story.
From the moment I could talk I was ordered to listen.
Now there's a way and I know I have to go away.[7]
–Cat Stevens

My first journey away from the US was in early 2003 when I took a leap of faith and decided to try out for the PBA. My father, as I mentioned, was a professional basketball player in the Philippines in the league preceding the PBA. I grew up under the heavy weight of his expectations. He was both my harshest critic and my most avid supporter but the pressure to succeed that he placed on me was intense. My whole life, up to that point, had been devoted to either getting away from him or earning his approval and my journey to the Philippines presented me with the opportunity to do both.

Growing up around my father was not easy. I waited in terror for the sound of the garage door opening as a child. I knew that when my dad got home, he would bring with him a heavy cloud of volatility and his fiercely demanding temperament. I had always excelled at basketball and I enjoyed it, but my dad, more often than not, managed to take the fun right out of it. Once, after a big victory in high school, my dad refused to allow me to join my team at the celebration because I had played poorly, at least according to his standards. The rigid and sometime cruel discipline which bordered on meanness both drove me and discouraged me.

Looking back at my journey, I realized that a lot of the insecurities I felt as a professional basketball player stemmed from this unhealthy relationship with my dad. Coach Tim Cone, he of the vaunted Triangle Offense, was my first head coach and I began my stint on his team desperately seeking his approval, just as I had with my father. When I continued to receive little or no playing time, I began to resent Coach Cone and reacted as a rebellious teenager might rather than as a professional player and as an adult. I forced myself to stop caring and focused my

---

[7] Stevens, Cat. "Father and Son." *Tea for the Tillerman*. Island/A&M, 1970.

energies on the primary methods of escapism available to me at the time: drinking, partying, and trying to get with women.

I was familiar enough with the behavior to know I was repeating patterns that had begun at an early age. As a young player for St. Joachim Elementary School in Hayward, California, I developed a habit of continually looking for my father in the stands to see how he was reacting to my performance. I was so afraid of the tongue lashing that I would receive from him if I messed up that I struggled to concentrate on anything else and, ironically or perhaps expectedly, played worse than if I not given any thought to my performance. The behavior continued as I grew up and my coaches noticed. Once, during a big game for my middle school, the coach of my team who knew me well, pulled me aside and warned me sternly, "if you look for your dad one more time, you're not going to play for the rest of the game."

My performance was always fear-based, which made my game tight, as in uptight, agitated, and characterized by nerves. My fear of failure and disappointing my father inhibited my abilities but my practice regimen and innate athleticism compensated enough to keep me on the teams I played for. When I was in the 10th grade, I made the varsity team for my high school but didn't get to see much court time because of the juniors and seniors playing ahead of me. Making varsity as a sophomore was a real achievement and a rare feat but my dad stopped coming to the games and my triumph began to feel more like a defeat. My father never said so, but I knew he was disappointed that I was not a more important part of my team's offensive production.

I continued to hone my skills and my game improved as I started my college career at Chabot College, a community institute and junior college in Hayward. It was there though, that I really let my Automatic Negative Talk or ANT--I even developed an acronym for it--get the best of me. My game had gotten good enough that I was attracting attention and getting offers from Division 1 colleges in the US NCAA. However, since I didn't fare well in school as a result of my learning difficulties, my GPA had become a major issue and I wasn't able to take advantage of any of these offers. I had always believed that basketball was the only thing I was good at and I had stopped trying academically. Sadly, this meant I lost out on better basketball opportunities down the road.

At Chabot College and away from the crippling scrutiny of my demanding father, I played very well. I even dropped 41 points in a single game but I felt a strong bias against Asian players. This feeling has been validated by players like Jeremy Lin who spoke out about facing the same obstacle. No matter how many points I scored or how many rebounds I pulled down and even if I was one of the strongest players in the game, I was always going to labeled as "unathletic" or "not powerful enough." While I was quietly helping our team win games, I was overshadowed by my more athletic teammates of different ethnicities. I made name for myself as a lanky "Asian Destroyer" but even that title held unspoken prejudice. "You played well," people said but I always wondered if they followed that up in their minds with the silent addendum *for an Asian.*

At least I was making a name for myself. Pleased with the attention I was receiving, my father began to attend my games again and the desperate search for his approval continued. Years later, in my first PBA game in Manila, my dad made a point to fly out to watch in person. We went up against a team called Sta. Lucia and I played about 10 minutes in that game although I can remember looking up at my dad every time I ran down the court. Being a rookie in the PBA, I didn't really try to force my will on offense. I looked to facilitate and make the right pass when I touched the ball, still establishing myself as a team player and an ally on the court. My dad wasn't happy about this and all he saw was that goose egg next to my name in the box score.

My dad returned to California and, in his absence, I subconsciously found his replacement for demanding father figure in my head coach, Tim Cone. As I did with my father, I began looking to him when I ran up and down the court. I beat myself up for even the smallest mistakes that I thought he might have detected. I beat myself up for not being used in games and attributed my lack of playing time to all those errors from the previous game. And then I would resent the coach as the cause of my distraction and therefore my mistakes: *If he would just get off my back…* This unhealthy cycle of blaming myself and resenting my coach went on for three full seasons.

Instead of determining what I could do to improve my basketball game and putting in the extra time in practice, I coped with my benching by partying the nights away. I developed the bad habit of going out every weeknight and blowing large portions of my paycheck on drinks and trying to impress other people in Manila's wild social scene. Looking back, I knew that this was an act of rebellion on my part. I knew that the root issue was the feeling of insecurity I had because, no matter how well I played, it would never be enough for my dad or any other father figure in my life.

They say that there is a thin line between love and hate and there were times when I truly hated my father but I never confronted him and certainly never said it to his face. I never really even rebelled while I was living under his roof or in the same country but, in my desire to please him and in my eagerness for his approval, I ended up resenting him. I knew that I was never going to be good enough for this living testament to the macho culture. I dealt with that realization by trying to cover up my supposed deficiencies with something else, anything else, actually.

This led to some major problems when it came to my career as a professional basketball player. I suppose the sort of behavior I was exhibiting would be detrimental to any profession but it was particularly toxic for one that demanded both physical stamina and mental awareness. I was acting far from professional, always coming in unprepared for practices and games, abusing my body by staying up late and pushing my tolerance level for alcohol and other substances. Predictably, like so many other pros who have crashed and burned in major leagues, I didn't last very long. My three-year rookie contract expired without renewal.

***

Despite all odds, as an unwanted and undistinguished free agent, I was able to find a new place on a new team and something clicked inside me. Losing my job had brought up a lot of raw emotion and feelings of inadequacy but, somehow, I was able to overcome that or use it to become a key cog on a title contender in the span of a few months. I signed a short-term contract but there was quickly talk about a longer, more lucrative extension and I felt like I had finally found my place.

I began channeling all the rage and frustration I felt for my dad into my game. It felt like I had finally been unleashed after three years of languishing on Coach Tim Cone's bench. I had a new lease on life. I was physical and unrelenting. No one was going to grab a loose ball away from me, no matter what the cost was. Unfortunately, the cost was my ability to ever play basketball or lead a normal life again.

On the play in which I was hurt, I was pursuing a loose ball. I got that ball seconds before Mick Pennisi came crashing down on my future. I only knew how to play one way. It didn't matter that I was picking up garbage stats in the fourth quarter of a blowout—my whole life was about turning garbage into something beautiful at that point just to show my dad.

I remember when my other family members flew over to see me in the hospital after a few days of arranging documents and long flights from California to Manila. Predictably, my mother was distraught. In the moments before I boarded the plane to Manila for the first time, my grandmother had prophesied over me. She had said gravely, ominously even, "You might get hurt," and, as I lay there on the floor shortly after Mick Pennisi fell on me, I thought about her words. My mother recalled those words as well and felt that perhaps we should have heeded the warning.

There was no way we could have known what would happen. People make predictions and give warning all the time and we never know which will come back to haunt us when our lives play out in a certain way. It leads me to consider how careless we sometimes are in speaking words that alter the directions of someone's life. I don't know if my grandmother was predicting the exact incident that occurred but I do know that words have power and what we say matters as does what we choose not to say. And while my family wept and lamented my accident, my father stayed silent. He wore that Stoic Mask to perfection, standing next to me by the gloomy hospital bed, making it impossible to know what he was thinking.

Of all the betrayals I had experienced and all the emotional damage inflicted by that man throughout my life, his stoicism in those moments was by far the most hurtful. When I moved my toe for the first time, I wanted him to cry. I wanted him to tell me that he loved me. I wanted him to lie to me and promise that "everything is going to be okay, Son." I didn't get any of those things. Instead, I saw him run to the bathroom so that no one would see him cry but I wanted to see him cry. I needed to see him cry for me. I needed to know that I had affected him as greatly as he affected me. I swallowed my rage and bitterness but I wanted to yell and scream at him: "SAY something! DO something! SHOW something!"

I was at the end of my rope. Everything I had ever worked for had been taken away from me. Earlier in the year, I had bucked the odds and gotten a second chance with a new team but there was no bucking the odds with this injury. There would be no second chances. I had to tell myself to accept my fate. And somehow, through the pain, agony, and confusion, I did. I knew on some level that I would someday make peace with all that had happened to me but I could not, for the life of me, understand how this man who raised me, who gave me everything I had, who I had tried to emulate for the last two decades, could not even shed a tear for me.

***

Time heals all wounds along with the frustration and anger that come with those wounds. That day, when I moved my toe for the first time, I witnessed my dad summon all the strength he had to hide his crying from me and I realized that I could not change him. It took me a while to learn that I could change myself though and that reconciliation would be possible because of that. While there are still plenty of things left for my dad and me to work on, I have learned to approach our relationship differently.

I changed. I stopped wearing my Stoic Mask and I allowed myself to be open and vulnerable. I "manned up" and took responsibility for my failures. I stopped blaming my father for making me want to be like him and for making me want to be perfect. I accepted that I would never be either of those things and that if I could live with that, then he could too.

I then I did what any maturing individual would do: I forgave him. I considered that he was a product of the hard life he had lived. He moved to the United States of America to give my brother, sister, and me a better life--the best life possible. He gave up his career as a professional basketball player for us and he was overwhelmingly hard on me because, in his own way, he wanted to make sure that I was making the most of the opportunities I had. He had done his best to give me the best and expected the same in return.

Seeing him in this light made my heart go out to him. I knew that deep down he was just a man who had been given a cultural code to follow at a young age and who hadn't been shown any other way. In Southeast Asia in the 1960s and 1970s, people didn't talk about their emotions. There had been no incentive to open up and every reason not to. He simply and blindly chose to follow the culturally accepted "best practices" of his day.

Yet here was a man who had a personal dream that he let die in favor of new dreams for his family. He left the Philippines and immigrated to the USA so that he could raise a son who would one day accomplish more than he himself could. He traded his dream for mine so could I really fault him for the intensity with which he watched my performance?

Perhaps it was this trade off that he had made all those years ago that he was thinking of when he looked at me in that hospital bed. Perhaps he was speechless in speculation--did he do the right thing by leaving the Philippines? Did he do the right thing pushing me to succeed, letting me move away from California to pursue my dream? Was he wondering if it was his fault? Maybe he had noted the circular sort of irony the situation presented: he had moved away from the Philippines to give me a better life and the ability to pursue my dreams which in turn led me back to the Philippines where the dream, his and mine, ended. As Marty McFly said in *Back to the Future*, "That's heavy, Doc."

***

When I first set out to write a book, I assumed that somewhere in it there would be a chapter bashing my father and calling him out on everything he did wrong while he was raising me. I had a list of faults and flaws at the ready as ammunition and a catalogue of every grievance. Eight years into this process though, I realized that this anti-Dad chapter would likely turn out to be the opposite. In planning out what I would write, I began to gain greater insight and understanding into my father's motivations and character and I knew then that this would be a chapter to honor my father, not criticize him.

I want to honor my father by pointing out principles that will serve as reminders to sons and fathers in pain that things can be better if they follow these guidelines and rules:

1.) **Do not wait until it is too late to verbalize your affection towards each other.** In my case, I am extremely fortunate that the accident did not end my life. I could have died there on the floor on that fateful day in May, 2006. I am glad that I am here to fix my relationship with my father and to tell him how much he truly means to me.

2.) **Do not fall prey to the vicious cycle.** It is said that angry fathers beget angry children, who end up producing furious grandchildren. I chose to stop the cycle. Never will I wear the Mask of Stoicism as a way for me to avoid pain and I won't take out my anger on my twin boys. I have forgiven my father and will follow a different path with my own children.

3.) **Realize that we are all imperfect and that we are all a work in progress.** My dad was a man who was shaped by hard choices. He made difficult decisions because he loved his family. This does not make him a villain by any stretch of the imagination. We both needed to fix a lot of things in our lives and we're probably not done fixing them yet but we are family and there is love there.

4.) **At the end of the day, there are very few things more sacred than the fundamental relationship between father and son.** It is through my earthly father that I discovered how my Heavenly Father loves me. In the Bible, the Lord declares, "For I know the plans I have for you, plans to prosper you and not to harm you, plans to give you hope and a future[8]." I can only imagine that my Dad had all these plans for me. He wanted me to make it big. For a brief moment, I was right there. I was living both his dream and mine. My Heavenly Father, however, had greater plans for me. I will say this in no uncertain terms: The impact I made in pro basketball was largely minimal. The impact that I will make in the world, however, is something more profound and significant. Through my paralysis, I will inspire people to fix fractured relationships everywhere. I am the living embodiment of the idea that what was once broken can be made whole and proof that we can move from our own prisons and paralysis into a free and fulfilled life.

---

[8] Jeremiah 29:11, The Holy Bible: New International Version, NIV. (Biblica Inc. 1973, 1978, 1984, 2011).

So, if you are reading this, Dad, know that I love you with my whole heart. It doesn't matter if you don't say it back to me. I see now that you have loved me this whole time and tried to show it in the ways you knew how. I want us to continue building our relationship because you have always been my hero and you always will be. Don't worry about the things that happened in the past. They happened for a reason and you are one of the biggest parts of my story. I will never know how much you have cared for our family. I will never truly comprehend the sacrifices you had to make for us but I know this, Dad, we will both be more than we ever intended to be. I love you. I will always be a Daddy's boy.

CHAPTER 7
"BACK TO LIFE"

The days at the Makati Medical Center in Manila were long and it didn't seem like I was making much progress. After moving my big toe in my huge breakthrough surgery, my improvement stalled. I was unable to regain movement in other parts of my body. The doctors in Manila were still very pessimistic about the possibility of me walking again. They gave me a 4% chance of doing so but I knew in my heart that I could achieve this feat. I had been told before that I would not be able to do something and then rose to the challenge, taking everyone around me by surprise.

There were several factors at play in the hospital in Manila that became a detriment to my recovery. The first factor was my celebrity status. My paralysis had been broadcast on a nationally televised basketball game and so I became a sort of "must see" presence when I was recovering at Makati Medical. Celebrities--actual celebrities--who were in the same hospital or visiting it, made a point to stop by my room. I met many interesting actors, politicians, and businessmen but this attention had the negative effect of altering the way the hospital staff approached me. They treated me with special consideration, pampering me, as it were. It sounds great but the end result was that they let me off easy. No one dared push me to get to the next level. I knew I had to get to get out of there if I wanted to take my recovery further.

I told my family that I needed to get back to California if I had any chance of ever walking again. By August 2006, four months after the accident, I was only able to move my arms and curl my biceps back and forth. I was not able to move anything below that aside from a few toes. Complicating the matter was my standing with my team, the Purefoods Chunkee Giants. They had been very supportive about my whole ordeal and had done what they could for me financially. I had signed a waiver excluding them from liability so they didn't have to pay my hospital bills but they did give me some money as a sort of ongoing salary to offset the costs. They wanted me to get better. I talked to the team officials and I asked for their blessing to go and do my recovery in the US. They agreed to pay me a final severance and wished me luck.

My financial prospects were not looking great. I knew that I would be digging myself into a deep financial hole if I went back and did my therapy in California. I researched a lot of places and, in the end, I knew that it would be best for me to do my rehab in a hospital where the staff would push me and didn't treat me like a celebrity. I enrolled in a place called SCI-FIT, the SCI being an acronym for Spinal Cord Injury and the FIT standing for Fitness. They set me up for an initial recovery at a hospital and then transitioned me into a gymnasium-like rehab facility afterward. I won't bore you with the financial details but let's just say that all the money that I received as severance from Purefoods was used up within a single month at SCI-FIT. It was all worth it though if it gave me a shot at mobility.

On August 18, 2006, four months and five days after my accident, I flew back to the US and began working towards my new dream: walking again. I closed the Philippine chapter of my life and turned my back on all the glamor and allure of Manila high-society with a new objective in mind. All I wanted at that point was to be a regular guy, living a normal life. It sounded like heaven and I was looking forward to the challenge.

***

Rehabbing at SCI-FIT was not an easy endeavor. I put in a lot of blood, sweat, and tears to make my first steps a reality. I was treated like a member of the US Marines. The nurses and therapists showed me love but it was the kind of love that you got from a drill sergeant. I made it through the tough days by looking forward to a time when my girlfriend would visit me from Manila.

Months of therapy went by and soon enough, in November of the same year, my then-girlfriend was able to take a break from her busy schedule. I was like a kid on Christmas Eve awaiting her visit. She met me at the hospital and I was overjoyed to see her. All the warm moments with her were still locked inside my memory bank and I felt like her coming over to see me was a step towards creating a new life together in the face of my changed circumstances. I was going to be able to live my normal life after all with her by my side, or so I thought.

On her visit, she brought with her a mutual friend of ours who ran in the same social circles in Manila. He was in the US to visit his child and the child's mother, who happened to be in San Mateo. I was very friendly and cordial to him and considered it an honor that someone from so far away would take the time to drop in and wish me well in my recovery.

The time with my girlfriend wasn't entirely easy. I carried a lot of frustration about what had happened and I knew that she was also struggling with the stress of the situation. I was sad when she told me she had to leave to get back to work but it had been so wonderful to be close to her again that I didn't really mind if it would be months until we were able to reunite. I thought about the old saying "absence makes the heart grow fonder" and I thought that if I fought hard enough, I could make the long-distance relationship work.

For one of her last weekends in the US visiting me, my girlfriend made plans to go to Las Vegas. She said she was going to meet up with a few friends there and I thought nothing of it at the time but eventually something inside me became restless. That mutual acquaintance of ours kept popping into my mind and doubts started to grow. I pressed her for more details on who exactly she planned to meet up with in Vegas and she rattled off a few names but did not include this friend of ours.

***

There's a popular Stevie Wonder song that goes *I'm a man of many wishes, hope my premonition misses.*[9] My premonition did not miss. I found out from my network of friends that this mutual acquaintance did make the trip to Las Vegas with my girlfriend. I confronted her about the situation

---

[9] Wonder, Stevie. "Lately," *Hotter than July.* Motown/Tamla, 1980.

as soon as I found out but she adamantly denied it. Pictures eventually surfaced on social media and my suspicions were confirmed. I felt like a lame-duck boyfriend waiting to be replaced.

My girlfriend went back to the Philippines along with the mutual acquaintance. She never admitted that she was seeing him but my head knew what my heart didn't want to accept. I kept trying to keep our relationship alive. I called her day after day. Our conversations were characterized by confrontation and denial. She never once admitted that this other man was part of the equation but she didn't have to. I knew. I just wanted desperately to hear that I was wrong.

One day, I made some really big progress at SCI-FIT. The drill sergeant-style training paid off, as well as the tens of thousands of American dollars I had spent in the place, and I was able to finally stand up with the help of the parallel bars. I did it all by myself and I was so proud of what I had been able to accomplish. I had come a long way and had proven my instincts were correct. I was about to show those doctors in the Philippines that they had been wrong and I was ecstatic.

My sister Dana took me and the rest of my family to a waffle place to celebrate my monumental milestone. I remember that day as one that started off on a high note but quickly fell apart. Just as I was about to dig into a feast of waffles in celebration of my being able to stand up again, my cell phone rang. My girlfriend's number came up on the screen.

I answered the call and I was about to yell into the speaker, sharing all the excitement I felt that morning, when I realized that it wasn't her calling me. Our mutual friend, probably trying to make a point and put an end to the calls I kept making to the woman who was now apparently his girlfriend, or at the very least, a friend with benefits, had called me in the middle of having intercourse with her. I could hear the moans and other sounds from half a world away.

I dropped my fork when I heard what was going on. My appetite disappeared and I felt sick. My heart was broken but I still couldn't accept that it was over. For a whole month after the waffle house phone call, I called her, hoping to win her back. I left messages and texted and ran up my phone bill in an attempt to restore what we once had, but it was no use.

A month after I got that phone call, I happened to tune into a TV show that was airing in the Philippines and saw my girlfriend. She was being interviewed and the host asked her how I was doing. She told them that I had changed as a person. She said that she still wanted to be with me but that I had become a monster impossible to have a relationship with. I knew then that the end had come (come and gone by the looks of it). She didn't announce the name of our mutual friend on national television but I knew that she was already with him. I accepted it but was so devastated by the loss and betrayal that I considered killing myself.

***

My then-girlfriend went on Philippine national television and renounced me publicly. It was humiliating and it was heartbreaking. I glanced around the room and saw a stash of pain medication near my bedside. I decided right then that I would take the pills and end the pain once and for all. I can't exactly explain what happened next other than to say that God had a plan and suicide was not part of it. My ex-girlfriend did one last thing for me. For some reason, she called my dad and asked him to look out for me because she was afraid that I was going to commit suicide. How she knew, I will never understand.

As my dad was rushing to my side, full of concern, I had already determined my course of action but I never got to the point of placing the pills in my mouth. I had the bottle of pills in my hand but, before I could take the life-ending overdose, I fell into a sort-of trance. I drifted off into the most realistic dream that I have ever experienced in my life. It was clear and vivid enough that I would almost call it a vision.

I dreamt about my own funeral. I saw my mother weeping at the sight of my body in the open casket. I saw my father, my brother, and sister—all of them were inconsolable because I had chosen to take my own life. I saw how my plan hurt the people who loved me. I woke up from the dream and decided that I couldn't go through with it after all.

My dad soon arrived and made a point of removing my access to medications of that sort but I had already come to the conclusion that I needed to find a way to get better. I knew that I needed the help of the Messiah, the one who I openly questioned when I got hurt. Jesus spoke to me during that dream. There were certain conditions I had to meet in order to get better, in order to heal fully. God led me to a passage in scripture that captured what I had to do in order to get well.

> *"Jesus stepped into a boat, crossed over and came to his own town. Some men brought to him a paralyzed man, lying on a mat. When Jesus saw their faith, he said to the man, 'Take heart, son; your sins are forgiven.' At this, some of the teachers of the law said to themselves, 'This fellow is blaspheming!' Knowing their thoughts, Jesus said, 'Why do you entertain evil thoughts in your hearts? Which is easier: to say, 'Your sins are forgiven,' or to say, 'Get up and walk?' But I want you to know that the Son of Man has authority on earth to forgive sins.' So he said to the paralyzed man, 'Get up, take your mat and go home.' Then the man got up and went home. When the crowd saw this, they were filled with awe; and they praised God, who had given such authority to man[10]."*
>
> -Matthew 9:1-9:8

This story from the Bible is my story. It has come true in my life both physically and metaphorically.

***

Spinal cord injuries are tricky things to maneuver around to say the least. Certain therapeutic enzymes or molecules need to be sent to the spinal cord in order to start the process of regeneration[11]. A specific condition has to be there in order for the regenerative process to begin. In other words, I had to create the ideal environment internally before the healing process could start.

My physical healing and restoration didn't begin until I let go of the bitterness in my heart. Having the prime years of my life and my livelihood taken away from me was a hard thing to get over. There was a part of me that wanted to stay down and wallow in self-pity. I wanted to become a victim instead of a victor.

---

[10] Matthew 9:1-8, *The Holy Bible: New International Version, NIV* (Biblica Inc, 1973, 1978, 1984, 2011).

[11] healtheuropa.eu/endparalysis-spinal-cord-injury/83539

I had heard of a concept called "learned helplessness" before. It was explored in detail by psychologists Martin Seligman and Steven Maier in the late 1960s and early 1970s. Seligman and Maier, in their famous experiments, gathered dogs and divided them into three groups. I am sad to report that this experiment involved shocking the dogs and while the methodology is unfortunate, the results are interesting so please bear with me.

In Group 1, dogs were strapped into harnesses for a certain time and were not given any shocks. In Group 2, dogs were given electrical shocks that they could avoid by pressing a panel with their noses. The dogs in Group 3 were placed in the same harnesses and also given the shocks. The only difference was Group 3 dogs were given no way to avoid the shocks.

After the initial round of shocks, with Group 1 as the control group, the dogs were placed in a box with two chambers: one where they would receive a shock and a second where they would be safe. In order to move from one chamber to another and avoid the shocks, all the dogs had to do was to jump over a barrier. As expected, all the dogs from Group 1 were quick to figure out that they just needed to jump over the barrier in order to get to the safe chamber. Group 2 dogs also figured this out rather quickly and there was no noticeable difference between this group and the control group. What was interesting was that the dogs in Group 3 did not even attempt to avoid the shocks. Based on their experience, there was just no way to overcome them so they resigned themselves to their miserable fates: a perfect textbook example of "learned helplessness."

Studying this made me consider the mindset of the paralytic man who was brought before Jesus. While the piece of scripture may not directly state it, the paralytic man must have been willing to get better. He had to believe that this Messiah would make him whole again.

I thought about my initial response to the devastating news that my girlfriend had left me. It was a shock to the system and there was nothing I could do to avoid it. I imagined myself as a Group 3 dog, whimpering in pain, resigned to a life of helpless negativity and I decided that I could not tolerate a life lived in this condition. If I was ever going to be something more than a has-been basketball player, I would have to develop the same resilience that the Group 2 dogs showed in Seligman and Maier's infamous experiment.

When Jesus healed the paralytic man, he mentioned the forgiveness of sins. He linked external healing or healing of the body with internal healing or healing of the soul. I realized then that playing the victim meant I could not create the right environment for Jesus to heal me. You may get the idea at this point that I was big follower of Jesus and was constantly looking to Him for answers and solace. I have to confess that this was not the case. Up to that point, I wasn't even sure that I believed in Jesus and yet He continually came to me in my dreams and thoughts with Bible stories and verses that spoke to my condition.

His messages were coming through to me, loud and clear. I saw that, as long as I played the victim, I would be harboring bitterness in my heart. I needed to let go of all the pain that my girlfriend had caused me. In order to receive true healing, I would have to forgive her for what she did, as painful as it was. I would also have to ask for forgiveness for my own transgressions.

Back in Manila, I had not been living my best life. I wore all those masks and, after that terrible phone call, a few of them slipped back on. I had started using drugs again to numb the emotional pain as well as the physical. The Invincibility Mask was telling me that it couldn't hurt me in the long run. I had never really made amends in my heart for the things I had done when I was wearing the Libertine's Mask so some of the pain over my girlfriend cheating felt like karma for the carousing I did before I was injured. It hit me that I needed God's forgiveness for a lot of shortcomings.

I initially felt that I had earned the right to play the victim. I mean, come on, I was paralyzed. Didn't that give me a little leeway to enjoy the fact that people were feeling sorry for me? The universe had dealt me a pretty rough hand after all.

Finding the true road to recovery meant being able to take responsibility for my own brokenness. I may have been broken physically through no fault of my own but I was broken in many ways of my own making as well. One of the reasons I wrote this book was to inspire people who still play the victim when faced with adversity to seek new ways to move forward. True healing can never occur if you buy into victimhood.

The Lord healed me but he forgave my sins first. Before my physical body was restored, God had to restore my soul and spirit. I could not hang on to the negative emotions and energy that I used to garner pity as a victim. In order for the enzymes that promote nerve regrowth to be able to alleviate the factors responsible for the growth of scar tissue, I had to surrender my inner being to the one who makes all things new.

***

I don't know if many of you readers will experience the level of physical pain that I went through but I do know that all of you will experience trials and adversities in varying degrees at some point. That's just life. People you trust and love may betray you. You may suffer loss, material or otherwise. That's just the way this volatile and uncertain world operates.

In order to overcome all this, we must be the victor instead of the victim. We cannot let negativity affect the way we live our lives. If I had never forgiven my ex-girlfriend, I would not have been able to take back my power. She got the attention she desired by talking about her breakup with me on TV instead of in person. Her ego did not need the additional stroking that my obsessing over her and resenting her would have brought.

It is our choice to forgive and until we do, we will waste away in a state of paralysis, clinging to our bitterness and negativity like a drowning man to a sinking ship. In order to walk again, I had to make the choice to let go. I could not hang onto my desire to be with this woman or my anger over the way in which she had deserted me. I had to trust that God had something better in store for me. Looking back at this time in my life, I can safely say that God did an amazing job of blessing me with more than I could have hoped or asked for at the time. Occasionally, we have to force ourselves to let go of old things that are no longer right for our lives and find peace in our hearts so that our minds and our eyes can be opened to the promise of new and better things on the way.

"This was the last basket that I ever scored in my professional basketball career. One minute after this picture was taken, I was paralyzed."

"In 2014, this was the moment when I heard the sweet words: 'you may now kiss your bride.'"

"My family never left my side through this whole ordeal. Here they are rejoicing with me at my wedding."

"This was the first made basket of my PBA career. I remember our opponents clearly, we were playing against Shell. I also remember that the person guarding me was none other than Tony De La Cruz, who later went on to help me get my story out into the world."

"Here I am celebrating my first professional basketball championship with the Alaska Aces."

"I was picked 15th overall in the 2003 PBA Draft. My basketball dreams came true."

"This was my second year in the PBA. To my right is EJ Feihl, the gentle giant I had talked about in this book."

"I am walking down the aisle as man and wife with Andrea, blessed to be able to actually walk as opposed to having to roll down the aisle."

"Here I am being acknowledged for my recovery back in 2012. I felt the love and support from the PBA and the fans that day as the packed Araneta Coliseum in Manila gave me a standing ovation. This game, the Purefoods franchise versus Ginebra San Miguel is known as the traditional 'Manila Classico.'"

"This is the JERK Crew--the brothers who stepped up for me during my time of need."

"This was the time when I first met Andrea, back in the year 2004."

"This was the green dress that was just perfect for Andrea. She was my date to my cousin's wedding in 2004. Who would have known that we would have gotten married 10 years later?"

"I got to experience Hong Kong with my brothers Jimmy and Harvey in 2006 as Talk N Text and Purefoods played a PBA game there. We were all doing our best Bruce Lee poses."

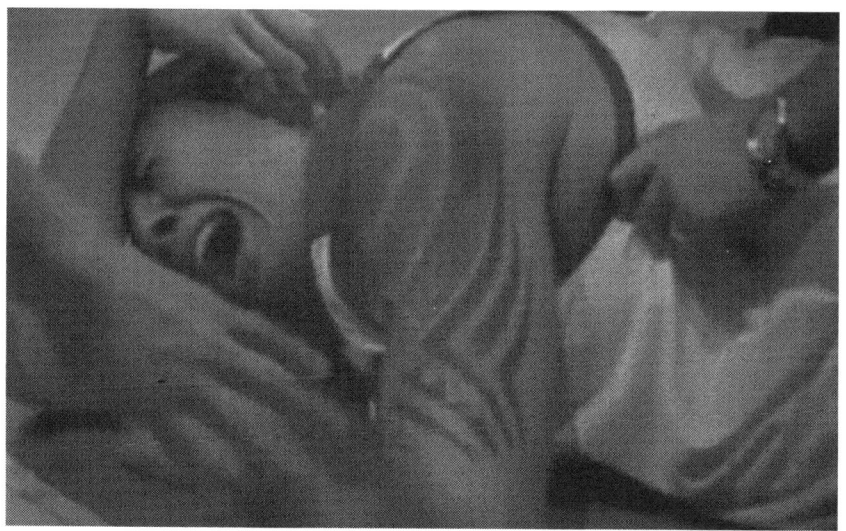

"The Moment I knew that my life would never be the same again."

"The PBA Draft Class of 2003."

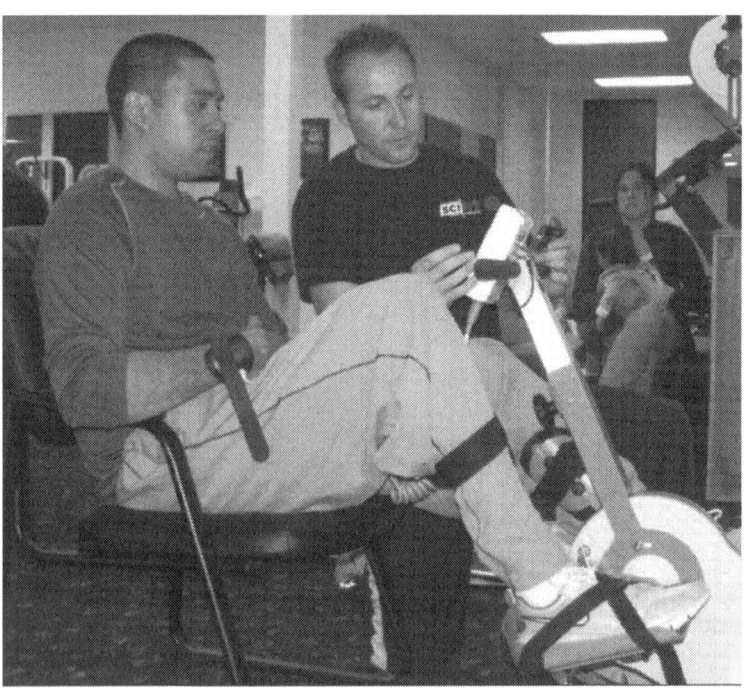

"I am thankful that SCI-FIT gave me the opportunity to push myself to heal."

"Here I am with my brother James and sister Dana during her high school graduation. This was the last graduation I was able to attend with her as she actually graduated from college on the same day that I was paralyzed."

"Ethan and Elliott Tejada-after my accident, I never imagined becoming a father, let alone a father to twins."***

CHAPTER 8

"FRIENDS AND FOES"

Once the thought of suicide had left my mind for good, I was able to fully focus on getting better. There were times, however, that it became difficult not to think about the many *what ifs* of my whole ordeal. I thought about the fateful night of my injury and the circumstances surrounding it. If someone were to replay that same moment a thousand times, 999 times out of a thousand what happened to me would not have occurred. In the movie *Any Given Sunday*[12], Al Pacino's character says, "football is a game of inches" and I couldn't help but think about the inches of my paralysis. If the ball had bounced one more inch to the left or right, Mick Pennisi might not have fallen on me and I would have carved out an amazing professional basketball career for myself.

I examined all the angles of the court in the Ynares Center. What if I had not been so aggressive in my attempt to reach my teammate's rebounding shot? What if that teammate never had possession of the ball? What if he had lost it to a member of the opposing team? What if he had seen a defender coming and passed it off instead? I replayed the scenario in my mind and just kept thinking about what I could have done differently and what Mick could have done differently. I kept wishing that any of those hundreds of factors involved in the play could have changed just slightly. I wished I had done anything other than jump for that rebound.

I never considered what Mick went through after that night in 2006. Deep inside, I guess I knew that he must have felt a tremendous amount of

---

[12] *Any Given Sunday.* Oliver Stone, Warner Brothers, 1999.

guilt, even it was a freak accident that he could have in no way predicted. It can't feel good to be part of a situation like that, to know you were the body, the driving force, that ended another player's professional career. Thinking about Mick made me consider several aspects of forgiveness that may not have occurred to me up to that point in time.

***

> *"I went over to have a civil conversation with Ali…But LaRusso kept butting in. I told him to get lost, 'mind your own business,' when out of nowhere the guy sucker punches me…I did what any dude would do, I defended myself. You know, I figured, that was that. But LaRusso wouldn't leave it alone."*
>
> -The character Johnny Lawrence in *Cobra Kai*

The *Karate Kid* was one of the most beloved inspirational movies of the 1980s. In the movie, Daniel LaRusso, an awkward teenager who has just moved to California from New Jersey, tries to fit in and start a new life. The movie was about him overcoming this bully, a guy named Johnny Lawrence. Daniel ends up "winning" Johnny's girlfriend, Ali, played by the lovely Elisabeth Shue.

People of my generation grew up rooting for Daniel LaRusso, as played by Ralph Macchio. We believed that he was the good guy and that Johnny Lawrence, played by William Zabka, was the ultimate bad guy. The quote above is from a scene in the spin-off television series *Cobra Kai*[13] where the supposedly villainous Johnny explains to his protégé his side of a 34-year long beef with Daniel *"Karate Kid"* LaRusso. It is interesting because in some ways Johnny's argument makes sense and it is a prime example of how there are always two sides to every story. Sometimes we get so caught up as the protagonist of our own story that we fail to consider what the people we are at odds with are going through.

We need to be careful who we paint as the villain in our lives and never forget that they are not two-dimensional movie characters designed

---

[13] *Cobra Kai*, "Strike First." Created by Josh Heald, Jon Hurwitz, and Hayden Schlossburg. Sony Pictures Television, 2018.

solely to forward the plot of stories in which we are the heroes. I spent a lot of years thinking of Mick Pennisi as little more than the dark force that set my tragic tale in motion, an antagonist if not a complete villain. I was angry at him and my anger blinded me to the tremendous emotional pain Mick felt because of what had happened.

Mick never intended for any of this to occur. Some people believe that he was pushed. I remember that as I was going for the rebound, Mick was jostling for position behind me. It was an awkward rebound and he lost his balance or was pushed and down we went. Mick's reputation as an enforcer and a dirty player made it easy for Philippine basketball fans to blame him for what happened or assume that his aggressive playing might have had something to do with how badly things turned out. Keep in mind, Mick is 6'9" and a true heavyweight. If anyone could be hired to play a supersized villain in a future James Bond movie, it would probably be Mick. Mick was aware of all this and he felt the judgment of the country along with his own guilt.

I didn't find out how much the incident had hurt Mick until I met up with him in 2012, six years after the accident happened. The co-author of this book, my writing partner and friend Mark Chan, ended up interviewing Mick alone as I had to leave the room. Mick was still so affected by the events of the game that my presence was hindering his ability to speak about the incident and its aftermath. Mick told Mark about the unfair heckling he received in the days after the accident. He also spoke about how he was handling it all pretty well until one random fan, a security guard at a bank in the Philippines, saw him one day and made a throat-slitting gesture followed by a thumbs up sign. That's when he lost it. He ended up screaming at the security guard and telling him that it was never his intention to hurt me that way.

I had been so focused on my side of the story that I hadn't considered what it was like to be the other person involved in the accident, the one dealing with survivor's guilt. In the months after the accident, I struggled to forgive two people: my ex-girlfriend who left me in the midst of my paralysis, and Mick. I even had revenge fantasies. However, sitting in my living room on that interview day in 2012, Mick was anything but a villain. He came across as sincere, genuine, and unexpectedly vulnerable.

I stopped seeing him as an adversary that day because I could feel how the event changed his life for the worse too.

Mick had been dealing with his own emotions and a lack of understanding from Philippine media, who were guilty of sensationalizing the event in order to generate ratings. During the interview, Mick spoke to my co-author about how much he respected and cared for me as a person. He actually broke down in tears when he explained how worried he was that he had put me and my family in a bad situation. He understood that I had lost my livelihood because of the accident. He also knew that I would never again play basketball. As a player himself, he knew what the sport mean to me and how much I loved the game. All these years, I thought he was just a miserable ogre who couldn't care less about what had happened to me.

***

I'm just going to put it out there: *Cobra Kai* is such a good show. If you were a fan of the original Karate Kid movies, you really need to see it. In one of the most fascinating scenes in *Cobra Kai*, Daniel and Johnny end up having a drink together. It felt so similar to when Mick came over to see me at my home. In that moment, I stopped viewing Mick as a caricature. He became flesh and blood, a person who had emotions that I had not even considered. I learned a couple valuable things from this encounter.

The first thing I learned is that forgiveness is a lot easier when we consider the other person's perspective. Evil exists in this world and there are some people out there who intentionally cause other people harm but most people, even those who might commit what some would consider bad acts, are not truly evil at their core. What I am saying is that forgiveness becomes easier when we force ourselves to view the world through the other person's eyes. When we consider what they have gone through and what pressures they may have felt, we achieve a more balanced view. This doesn't mean that we have to give up our stance on the matter or betray our principles, it just means that we remove the potential to overreact and to oversimplify the issue.

Forgiving Mick allowed me to focus my energies on inspiring others. Do I wish the accident never happened? Sometimes, yes, but honestly, I can say that the accident happened for a reason and it made me a better person. I would not be in a position to change the world like I am today if

I had not become paralyzed. All I wanted in my youth was to be the best professional basketball player I could be but now I have the opportunity to be so much more than that. As my life story unfolds, I am in a unique position to tell the world about the power of forgiveness and about focusing on what is truly important.

I could be telling a different story: one in which I am a tragic figure to pitied. I could paint Mick as the villain who took everything from me—the man in black in an old pantomime, twirling his handle-bar moustache and laughing cruelly. What a pathetic way to go through life. I learned that becoming a champion means being able to let go of the past and be present in the moment. All my energies are now focused towards inspiring people, not seeking their pity. There was a purpose for all the pain I went through. I believe that the Lord is going to use my experience to help bring healing into the lives of those who have suffered great loss like I have.

The second thing I learned from Mick's visit was that forgiveness takes the power away from the offending party. How many times in the age of YouTube and reality TV have we seen stand-offs where both parties could have easily gone their separate ways without injury or insult? Too often. No one ever really wins in a fight posted for the world to see. People risk criminal charges, the loss of employment if their bosses or future bosses see the fight online, and looking like a moron. Why don't they just walk away? It is because both parties have given too much power to the other person.

When we allow people to play the role of the super-villain and mistakenly bestow upon ourselves the tag of superhero (superheroes never ignore a call to arms), we fall prey to one of the biggest traps of self-indulgence around. The truth is, we can simply ignore the turmoil that goes on in the outside world and focus on creating peace within our inner world. In this day and age, inner peace is often sacrificed at the altar of public approval and validation. We are more concerned about getting people on our side than actually creating peace within ourselves and we'd rather be vindicated than happy.

By initially hanging on to the bitterness in my heart that I had for Mick, I gave him way too much power. My focus was outward rather than inward. When I was able to release those feelings of pain and hurt, I was able to see what was truly important and move forward in my inner growth, unimpeded by an unforgiving heart.

***

As I observe the pitfalls that society has presented us with at this moment in human history, I see a lot of the lessons that my paralysis has taught me being played out. Even after I was paralyzed, I still viewed myself as some sort of celebrity. I could not rid myself easily of the masks that I wore, even if my ability to walk again depended on it. It took me a lot of time to see it but I believe that the conservation of energy was what enabled me to finally defy the odds the doctors gave me and walk.

Initially, when I was hurt, I spent all my energy trying to think of ways to show that I was worthy of people's pity. I directed the energy outward towards other people instead inward towards my broken pieces and I realize now that this may have been the thing that kept me from being whole again for some time.

Modern life presents us with a great challenge: we must live in the way of truth in a day and age that peddles fallacy and deceit at an alarming rate. Many people today, young and old alike, are caught up in vicious patterns of energy depletion as they argue with each over social media and try hard to convince people that their lives are worth living instead of just living those worthy lives. We are constantly worried about what other people think of our narrative and use the medium for self-promotion and ego stroking. We think that the attention will make us feel happy, connected, and loved but in the end, it just makes us needy, lonely, and distant.

When we think too much of other people's views of us, we feed the part of our beings that want to be exalted all the time. We need to reject this urge and find true humility. The universe does not revolve around us. We are not heroes surrounded by supporting players and villains. My ability to heal would not have been unlocked as long as I remained a narcissist full of resentment for those around me. We have to forgive others because we are all imperfect creatures that need forgiveness for our mistakes. Doing this will open the door for many miracles in our lives.

***

In my mind I have a vision: it's like a commercial I see in my head but unlike most commercials, it's not trying to sell a product or a service. This commercial is designed to inspire people with an idea. I see this commercial taking place roughly 14 years since the accident. I am sitting in my wheelchair in the exact same spot on the court in the Ynares Center where the accident took place, the spot where my hopes and dreams were shattered.

I contemplate these things for a minute and then, in my commercial, I take out my crutches and I stand up. I take a few steps towards the baseline, right below the hoop the ball rebounded off of during that fateful game. I take another step and then one of my crutches breaks. In my vision, I can't use just one crutch. It is simply too hard. I don't know if I can make it to that baseline. I consider giving up and returning to my wheelchair.

As I am about to turn back, someone emerges from the locker room tunnel. He is a bald, 6'9" man with a villainous goatee. He takes my broken crutch from my hand, sets it aside, and puts my arm around his neck. He helps me take one step and then two. It's Mick and he and I share a moment together.

I have been significantly changed since the injury 13 years ago. Although I survived the accident, in many ways, the old Eugene Tejada died right there on that spot. I don't know for sure but the old Mick probably died on that spot as well. It is the new Mick who shares the moment with me in my vision. Together, we look directly above us at the basket: the metal ring, the stiff white netting. How many bodies have been sacrificed at this 10-foot altar? The question is unspoken but is somehow tangible for both of us at that moment.

Mick guides me a few more steps and we head into the locker room tunnel but not towards the locker room. We head towards the exit of the building. The gym is dark and dingy because it is noon in Manila and no one else is in the arena that seats 10,000 people aside from me and the fictional ogre. In that moment, the ogre has revealed that he is a noble prince. Mick and I make our way to the door, my left hand around his neck and my right hand still holding onto my crutch. I have left the wheelchair behind.

When we open the door, an almost blinding ray of sunlight hits us both in the eyes. I imagine that this was the same blinding light that hit Saul on the road to Damascus and began his transformation into Paul the Apostle. Mick and I blink and, when our vision returns, we look around and take in the beautiful scenery. We hear the birds overhead and a warm breeze rustling through the many trees around us. We look out over the hills of Antipolo that are awash in a vivid green chaos of plants and flowers and life itself.

As I am looking around, Mick whispers something. I am the only one who hears it and he didn't need to say it--I have already forgiven him. But I hear his words as we bask in the sunlight of noontime in the Philippines, perhaps the brightest sunlight that a human being can experience. I know he wants me to say something. He wants me to respond. He needs me to but there is only one appropriate response: "I'm sorry too, Mick." We stand in that moment, champions and conquerors, regardless of what the annals of PBA history will show. I look at him and there is nothing but mutual love and understanding between us.

CHAPTER 9

"RISK AVERSE"

I made slow but consistent progress at SCI-FIT and had several promising breakthroughs. Through it all, I hung on to my dream of walking again one day and I continued to push my body to cooperate. I let the tough love of the instructors and therapists at SCI-FIT motivate me and push me to work through any frustration and, before too long, I was released from the hospital setting and I returned to living with my mother.

Moving back home with my mother as a paralytic posed some serious challenges for me, particularly as they related to my self-esteem. Even if I had made progress in my therapy, I was still unable to perform many of the basic functions and tasks that a normal adult takes for granted. I moved into my mother's house and basically had to be treated as a baby again. My mother had to bathe me, clean me when I soiled myself, and she had to feed me: all the things she had done for me when I was an infant.

Life went on like this for some time and my mother continually reassured me that she would be there to care for me as long as she had to but it never occurred to her that I needed some reassurance that someday her care wouldn't be necessary. I needed to know that someday I was going to be able to fend for myself and that I would find a way to earn a living on my own. I needed to know that independence was possible. I love my mother very much and I appreciate all the sacrifices she was making to care for her grown son but I hoped to heaven that someday I would be able to walk out her door and into a fulfilling adult life.

To say that what happened to me in 2006 was difficult for my mother would have been a tremendous understatement. The fact that my paralysis occurred on Mother's Day of that year made it all the more painful for her. Immediately following the accident, she began to regret allowing me to pursue my dream. I had left my hometown in 2003, a wide-eyed explorer in pursuit of greener pastures with the dream of becoming a professional athlete. Just as I was starting to hit my stride, I was knocked down, reduced to an invalid dependent on the care of other people. It all happened in the blink of an eye. Now that I was back in her home and under her care, she had deep misgivings about allowing me to pursue my new dreams of walking and working again.

In my mother's mind, the last time I took a big risk I ended up as a quadriplegic. It was hard for her to see that I could not let one setback, no matter how large, define my life. I knew that I needed to take more risks if I was going to be the kind of person that would leave a lasting impact on this earth but my mother struggled to accept this. She wanted to hold onto her little boy and protect him from the world that had treated him so cruelly.

My mother encouraged me to stay at home and enjoy the benefits of our social systems, namely Social Security and disability insurance. I suppose if the system was ever built with someone in mind, that would be me. I would have had more than enough excuse to avail myself of these benefits but while it was a solid safety net, deep inside, my heart and soul could not accept it. It was the cautious option. The easy option. I knew that I needed to take risks. I had left the safety net created by the financial support Purefoods had offered me and I had left the comfort of celebrity status and the coddling at the hospital in Manila. It was risk taking that had gotten me this far. With great risk comes great reward and the reward I was looking for was not a cushy life being cared for by others--I wanted to walk.

***

"The biggest risk is not taking any risk…In a world that is changing really quickly, the only strategy that is guaranteed to fail is not taking risks."

–Mark Zuckerberg

In February 2015, during Superbowl XLIX, with the game clock winding down, the Seattle Seahawks made it all the way to the New England Patriots' one-yard line. There were 26 seconds left in the game and Seahawks quarterback Russell Wilson took the snap and passed the ball. The play resulted in an interception by Patriots rookie Malcolm Butler and the Seahawks lost the game and the championship 24-28. A score for the Seahawks at that juncture in the game would have most likely seen them win by a score of 31-28.

As someone who is not partial to either the Seahawks or the Patriots, it is very interesting to look back at this game because we can see all sorts of game theory applications and analysis of risk at play as we examine Seattle Coach Pete Carroll's decision. An explanation of the psychology behind the calls made by both coaches has significant relevance to the way I approached my personal decision to follow new dreams after my paralysis.

With a little over a minute left in this watershed game, Seattle had a first down at the five-yard line, meaning they were five yards away from scoring. All they had to do was march down the field five more yards—15 feet—and the game and championship would be theirs. Coach Carroll elected to run the ball with star running back Marshawn Lynch on the first down and he gained a quick four yards. The ball was now on the one-yard line. As many of you know, in football, the clock keeps ticking after a run is stopped and this is where both Coaches engaged in what was essentially a game of poker and clock management.

At the time, there was a trend in the league of coaches allowing the other team's offense to score with that much time left on the clock in order to put the ball back in the hands of their own offense while there was still time to make up some ground. Coach Carroll must have been expecting this as New England still had two timeouts left. It wouldn't be crazy to assume that the Patriots' master tactician, Bill Belichick, winner of three previous Superbowls, would stop the clock with a timeout, allow the Seahawks to score, and then place the ball in the hands of arguably the greatest quarterback in modern NFL history, Tom Brady.

However, this would mean that New England had only a minute or so left to score from kickoff. They would have to gain 80 yards in a span of 1 minute in order to win. My guess is that Coach Belichick elected to take his chances and bank on stopping Seattle 3 more times at the one-yard line. He ran his risk analyses and played the odds.

Seattle had no remaining timeouts. If they were stopped on a run play, they would have to spike the ball on the third down. This meant intentionally giving up a down to set up a play for the final try on the third down. Carroll hoped that Belichick would let him score but Belichick must have figured that this would be giving Seattle too much of an advantage. It wasn't going to happen.

The Patriots were already ahead and all they had to do was stop the ball in order to win. Coach Belichick knew that the faster the clock ran down, the more pressure Seattle would be under to call a play. He was aware of the trend in allowing offenses to score uncontested in order to get the ball back quickly but he wasn't going to concede 80 yards to Carroll when all he had to do was stop them 3 more times for one yard. From Belichick's perspective, the clock was actually on New England's side, even if it didn't appear that way to the casual fan watching at home.

Belichick anticipated that Carroll was expecting him to use one of his timeouts to hedge New England's risk. If Seattle scored, the Patriots would still have enough time to make a come-back. This is where the true risk lay. Belichick was risking Seattle scoring without leaving enough time on clock for his own offense to do what they needed to do. If the Patriots failed to stop Seattle on the one-yard line on their second or third down, it would be all over for the Patriots. Belichick was going to have to bet on his team's abilities and trust in his defense to win the game rather than putting the outcome in the hands of Tom Brady, the star player.

Belichick identified the risk he wanted to take, basically declaring "we're going to stop them or we're going to lose trying." He went all-in on this decision. Instead of calling timeout to stop the ball and to hedge his bet, he let the clock run. Perhaps hedging is only for mere mortals, not coaches who win multiple Super Bowls! As the seconds wound down, from a minute to 50 seconds, panic began to set in for the Seattle brain trust.

Now the time pressure was squarely on Seattle and Pete Carroll had to make one of two decisions. He could call for a pass or he could call for a run play. In a pass play, provided Seattle avoided an interception, they would essentially be getting a "free" play in that if the ball was dropped, the clock automatically stops and they wouldn't have to burn another down to get off 2 more potential plays to win.

I respect Pete Carroll as a coach but I think that, in this moment, he over-thought things and may have let Belichick get the best of him in the psychological game the two coaches were playing while their players battled it out on the field. Carroll wanted to leave himself a back-up option instead of going all in on a run play—a run play, aka "give the ball to Marshawn Lynch and let him jam it down the throats of the New England defenders." Belichick trusted his defense but Carroll seemed to doubt his offense in this crucial moment.

Marshawn Lynch is a very large human known for using his weight to bulldoze people. He earned his famous descriptor "Beast Mode" for his ability to use his size to gain yardage and, in this case, he only needed to gain one yard. On this, the most important play of the season for the team, Lynch's physical gifts seemed ideally suited to lead his team to victory. The only drawback was that calling a running play in this situation would have prevented Seattle from hedging. Running was risky because, on the off-chance that Lynch was prevented from scoring, Seattle would have to burn another down to get another chance to set up one more play for the win. Coach Carroll decided to try for a pass play first.

With time running out, Seattle quarterback Russell Wilson executed a pass play on command from his coaching staff and threw the ball to a player he thought was an open receiver. Instead, an undrafted rookie came up with the interception and the rest is history. The Patriots snatched victory from the jaws of defeat as the result of a risky play call--some say a Jedi mind trick-- from their head coach.

While I am not necessarily the biggest Bill Belichick or Patriots fan in the world (*Go San Francisco 49ers!*), I realize that Belichick was gutsy and took the road less travelled. He defied expectation and refused to play it safe. He won the game because he doggedly believed in his strategy and vision and got his opponent to blink first. After thinking about that play over and over again, I knew that I had to bet on myself just as Belichick had bet on defense. I needed to trust my vision for my life and not let the pressures of the outside world get to me.

When I was hurt, my mother was understandably very upset. Just as I lost my original dreams for my future, she lost her dreams for the kind of life her son would have. She wanted to care for me and make sure that I had what I needed in the worst-case scenario but her focus on preparing for the worst made it hard for her to dream of the best-case scenario. She felt that the safest thing for me to do was remain unemployed and collect the disability insurance. It was steady and we could make ends meet on the little that it paid. But, just like the play call that Pete Carroll had to make, while there were benefits to staying unemployed, there were also drawbacks.

I chose to analyze these life choices before me like they were plays in a sporting event. This was a familiar concept to me and helped me to make sense of the monumental decisions I was being faced with. My first option was the "Remain Unemployed" play and it involved letting my mom and the insurance company take care of me for the rest of my life. The benefit to this play was that I wouldn't have to work ever again. And, hey, why not go that route? It's not like I *wanted* to be paralyzed. It wasn't my fault that I ended up this way. I could just milk the system and continue with my low-key existence.

The drawback to this option or play--the risk--was that I would be choosing a defeatist attitude and giving up my own agency. And while it may not have been directly my fault that I was paralyzed, I still needed to take responsibility for myself and move on regardless of the tragedy. Relying on external forces to care for me *ad aeternum* would take the *locus of control* out of my hands.

The locus of control is an interesting concept developed by Julian B. Rotter in 1954. It is the degree of control people believe they have over their lives and the outcome of events in their lives. It's a belief inside ourselves that what we do can make a difference. We increase our locus of control when we stop playing the victim. A person with a strong locus of control takes responsibility for their circumstances and understands that their reality is something that they helped shape with the decisions they have made. I knew that I needed to take responsibility for my life again. It was not my fault that I was paralyzed but, at the same time, it would have been my fault if I allowed the paralysis to keep me down.

My second option was the "Try to Make Something of Yourself" play, also known as the *shoot for the stars--rejection and failure be damned* play. If successful, I could get back to a place where I could dream of living alone, buying my own home, or doing something inspirational like writing a book or touring and giving motivational speeches. This play sounded amazing but had its drawbacks as well.

What if I tried but wasn't successful enough? By working I would prove that I no longer needed the insurance payments and would lose that money but there were no guarantees that whatever job I found would pay enough for me to live off of and cover my medical costs. There would be no second chances so it was a very risky option.

Eventually, like Belichick in that fateful final minute of the Superbowl, I decided to take the risk and forget about hedging my bets. I bet on myself like Belichick bet on his defense. The real risk, in my mind, was to allow myself to sink deeper into victimhood. We've all been there before, doubting our ability to reach our goals and making every excuse we can so that we can remain on the safe path. What we don't realize is that sometimes, the safe play can be the riskiest call of all.

Pete Carroll opted for the safer play and it failed. He probably second guessed himself a million times following that decision. I knew I didn't want to spend my life second guessing my choices. I would have to do what Pete Carroll had not done and go for broke. Ultimately the worst possible choice for me would be to play it safe, to allow myself to stay down. Even if I ended up walking again, what good would it do? I needed to be in a place where I could use my successes to inspire and help other people.

My mom is one of the most loving people I have ever come across. Her care and commitment know no bounds but, if there is any fault in her, it is that she is *too* loving. When I was hurt, she was there and she made me feel safe which was important because my world was crumbling around me and I needed someone to take me in and care for me. I found safety and solace in the loving arms of my mother.

There are fewer things in life tighter than the hold she had on me and I appreciated it but this secure hold would eventually suffocate me if I didn't remove myself when the time came. Just like the boxer who will never win a fight if he never attempts a single punch, I would never learn how to live again if I was not allowed to spread my wings and fly. I had to take a risk and move away from the safety she provided.

We have a tendency to play it safe sometimes. It's human nature and I'm sure it has contributed to the survival of our species but progress comes when we bet on ourselves, get a little uncomfortable, and take risks. Progress came when cave men first decided to use fire, something that must have been terrifying to them, as a tool. Progress came when the explorers set out for foreign lands. It wasn't safe and it wasn't comfortable for them. Often, we try to have it both ways. We want to win but we don't want to let go of our safety net. We opt for the play that gives us multiple chances and back up attempts instead of taking that one solid-but-terrifying, best shot.

The next time you're feeling pressured to play it safe, ask yourself: *what are the risks in this scenario and what are the rewards?* More often than not, the real risk involved is staying stagnant when you could, alternatively, go for it and make your shot count. I hope my journey will inspire others to take that leap of faith into the endzone in order to reap the glorious rewards that await.

CHAPTER 10
"BETTER SKILLED THAN SAFE"

Knowing that I didn't have to play the victim anymore liberated me. From the moment I made the declaration that I was going to work again and that I was going to walk using my own two feet, I was able to make amazing progress. Over the course of several months, I pushed myself to perform tasks that may have seemed mundane to anyone else but that for me were groundbreaking. One task that held particular importance was driving. The way the doctors in Manila had made it sound, this would be nearly impossible. However, I had already come so far and had been able to make one remarkable breakthrough after another that I thought, *why not? Why not this particular task?* I became determined to get behind the wheel again and dreamed of the new freedom and mobility that driving would bring. I would no longer be tethered to one place but could, in this way at least, move about the world again.

Learning to drive again was like facing a dragon. The first time I got behind the wheel after my paralysis, I was overcome with fear and couldn't bring myself to turn the key in the ignition at first. *What if I lose control of the vehicle and run over someone?* My mind played every worst-case scenario but I knew that the way forward would be to trust my instincts and believe in the progress I had made so far. I started the engine and the dragon roared to life but I knew that I could make it work even before I made my first turn.

Sure enough, driving turned out to be a skill that was manageable for me. My first few stints behind the wheel were more than a little scary but I got through them and, with the use of special hand controls, I was able to become quite proficient at driving. As I write this, I am currently working as an Uber driver. Back in California, I knew that driving would be a crucial skill to master in order to have a career again; I just didn't know that driving would actually become my career. I could never have imagined this for myself when I got injured 14 years ago. My success behind the wheel and the fact that I had almost allowed my fear to stop me from turning that car on reminded me that, if I planned to continue developing new skills, I would have to overcome the temptation within me to always play it safe.

In life, you have to be able to step out of your comfort zone and attack those dragons that leave you shaking with fear. Now, I am not advocating for taking crazy, mindless risks and acting on every impulsive idea that pops into your mind. I am talking about achieving what seems impossible by taking calculated risks based on a foundation of hard work and proven success at a microlevel. My recovery was contingent upon setting smaller goals for myself at the beginning and taking bigger risks only upon successfully achieving those small goals.

Before I could drive again, I first had to learn how to raise my own arms up and I had to learn how to consistently control them again. Sounds simple enough, right? We take for granted our ability to perform those regular, mundane chores of everyday life but, if there was one thing my paralysis taught me, it was to be thankful for being able to brush my own teeth or shower, or to be able to use a fork and knife again. All these average duties were small wins which I translated into confidence-building milestones that propelled me forward and made larger goals seem possible but, before setting bigger goals, I had to calculate the risk at each step.

Each accomplishment, however small, represented a huge investment of time and energy, both physical and emotional. Once I calculated that an objective's upside was worth the risk, I set out to reach that objective with the gritty determination of a hunting dog. I would start out by failing repeatedly. When I was first learning how to use utensils again, I dropped my family's silverware so often you'd think the set had been coated with butter. However, the more I tried and failed, the more determined I became to reach my objective because by then I had invested my heart and soul into accomplishing what I had set out to do.

> *"For those that say I endanger my child: it's more likely that you will fall while walking on the sidewalk than I will while skating with my daughter."* -
>
> Tony Hawk

It never fails to amaze me how people can look death in the eye on a daily basis. I'm talking about the fireman who rushes into the burning building and the Mixed Martial Artist who musters up the courage to face off against a human wrecking ball hell bent on destruction. I'm talking about professional skydivers who fall tens of thousands of feet down to earth in a matter of seconds, only to want to do it again on the very next ascent. These are dangerous activities but these are not careless humans. On the contrary, they are some of the most careful people on the planet.

Humans have an amazing ability to assess risk, decide if the reward is worth that risk, and then commit to their goals with their whole beings. To compete in the octagon, for example, an individual has to master at least three forms of martial arts that include striking (punching and kicking sports such as Muay Thai or kickboxing), some form of wrestling or grappling (jiu-jitsu, Greco-Roman wrestling, judo), and anything else in between. Countless hours are spent simply learning how to protect their own neck.

In one of the biggest ironies in life, my mother would not allow me to play football because she didn't want me to get hurt. Lying in that hospital bed in 2006, I thought about how I should not have let anyone stop me from playing a sport that I was excited to play because it was supposedly dangerous. No matter what we do, safety is never entirely assured.

Safety is a false concept. There is really no such thing on earth as an entirely safe place. Nor is there an entirely safe activity. People are injured pulling out a chair at the dinner table, in the shower, and in their own backyards. In fact, most accidents occur at home. For the most part we don't allow this fear to stop us from getting out of bed every day and living our lives normally but we do allow this fear to stop us from taking risks and living exceptional lives. I believe that each of us has been placed on earth with one life to live and we have to make those lives count without letting fear get in the way.

***

A person can cause just as much harm as good by encouraging safety in the wrong way. You can harm someone by requiring them to be less than they were meant to be and by denying them the tools required to be successful. This is why it is better to be *skilled* than *safe*.

When someone is crazy enough to want to fight in the UFC, it is probably futile for anyone to try to discourage this person by telling them that it is too dangerous. If their passion for fighting is strong enough, they will do it anyway—whether it is on the street or in the octagon. It is better then, to encourage them to train hard and learn how to defend themselves in the octagon. When a person is able to master skills and develop technique, they will have a better chance against their opponent and better odds of avoiding injury.

You don't need to look as far afield as professional martial arts to see how this principle of skill vs. safety can play out. If your child is obsessed with skateboarding and wants nothing other than a board for their birthday but you resist because of the risk, you are potentially setting your child up for even greater risk of injury. Chances are they will come across a skateboard at a friend's house or at the park and will be drawn to give it a try without the skills, practice, or safety equipment required. Wouldn't it be better to provide your child with a helmet, knee and elbow pads, and discuss the importance of building up their skill level in manageable increments while working towards larger goals like 360-degree hardflips?

Being paralyzed led me to the deep realization that life was never meant to be played safe. When I was hurt in the accident, my mother gave me the option to live out my days under her protection. I wouldn't have to worry about anything anymore; I would be safe from all of life's dangers and disappointments. To accept *this*, I realized, would have been true paralysis. Being in a wheelchair would have paled in comparison to the paralysis of the soul that would have come with succumbing to a spirit of mediocrity and passive acceptance.

When I was growing up, my mother sought to protect me from failure as much as she could. I was a slow learner so she would often take it upon herself to do my homework for me because she didn't want me to suffer failure. Her intentions may have been good but this approach did not serve me in the long run. I would have been better off learning to deal with the initial disappointment and using those experiences to motivate me to do better in my academics. Protecting me from these early failures actually prevented me from learning valuable lessons in coping and resilience. I had to develop these emotional strengths later in life. I had to learn that failing in a first attempt is not the end of the world but simply an opportunity to try again with more experience and knowledge.

As an adult and following my accident, I came to the realization that failure is merely the start of a new path and not the end of the road and so we all must ask ourselves a critical question in life: Have I let the fear of failure keep me from becoming excellent and following a new path? Many of us are currently stuck in this state. We live in our mother's basements--proverbial or actual basements. We stick with the same career for 30 years because we are afraid of what will happen if we dare to step outside our boxes and consider our greater purpose. Millions of dreams have been sacrificed and shattered at the altar of safety. Being paralyzed is a state of mind as much as physical condition and our collective obsession with security has led to paralysis of epidemic proportions.

Every day I meet people who tell me about something they've wanted to do for a long time. Many have dreams they wish they had the strength to follow. They have deluded themselves into accepting second best because this is "real life" and security is paramount. Occasionally, they opt for the safe choice because they received "advice" from another unhappy person who let his or dreams die along the wayside. Often, this person is a parent who was also sold on the safety-above-risk spiel and believed they must pass this message along to their children. This is how we allow the vicious, dream-killing cycle to endure from generation to generation. Instead of asking how we can be skilled, we have changed the question to how we can be safe.

***

"What are your plans for the future?"
"I plan to be an accountant."
"Oh, what made you choose finance?"
"My father was an accountant. His father was an accountant. It's a steady career that usually pays decent money."

"But is it something you really want to do?"

"Well, not really but I'm pretty good at it and it just kind of makes sense. I can get in with my dad's company and start paying off those student loans. If we're talking about what I really want to do, I've always wanted to sail around the world. I wanted to get my own boat and just circumnavigate the globe, you know, like Ferdinand Magellan and the old explorers did."

"Why don't you do that then?"

"Yeah right! Because this is real life and I have bills to pay. I'll make some money and maybe buy a boat when I retire, assuming I still have the strength and energy to learn how to sail."

Does this sort of conversation sound familiar? I know I've had this talk with any number of people. They reach adulthood and they walk into their solid, sensible careers, hanging their hopes and dreams on a hook by the door. Martin Luther King Jr. once said, speaking about Civil Rights, "a dream deferred is a dream denied." This wonderfully poignant observation applies to any dream. To opt for the status quo in favor of taking a chance on one's dream, shelving it for a future date, is to live in a construct of security and stability that can quickly become suffocating.

As I said, I have had the conversation above with many people. I have heard the same line of reasoning across various cultures and on different continents. I have met people who have devoted their lives to being safe but, at the same time, I have also met people who did not let anything stop them. They live their dream every single day. They fight for it and revel in it and put themselves out there, walking a fine line between ultimate personal fulfillment and complete devastation. And you know what, they love it. They wouldn't live any other way.

The message of this book is not to quit your job tomorrow, leave your friends and family behind, and head out to pursue that long-buried inner dream of becoming a nautical explorer. It is, rather, about re-evaluating the way you think about the world. Have you ever met someone you were really attracted to but were afraid to call them because you have somehow been conditioned to believe that they were out of your league? Have you ever taken a job you had a sneaking suspicion you were going to hate because you had bills due and needed a pay check and didn't think anything better would come along? Have you ever prevented yourself from asking for a promotion because of the possibility your boss might say no and you would feel embarrassed?

If the answer to any of the above questions was "yes" I would like you to listen to advice that comes from a man who lost everything and somehow gained it back and more—there is no time to engage in this debilitating form of self-pity and defeatism. In order to be all that we can be, we must be willing to take risks. We must build skills that will allow us to overcome potential drawbacks and not focus on what we can lose, only what we can gain. A person with nothing to lose often becomes the most powerful person in the room because that person does not let the fear stop them from taking a shot and giving it their best in any situation.

***

One of the things that I have come to despise about our modern culture is the proliferation of "trolls" on the internet. These on-line dream-killers are quick to give their toxic advice and encourage people to give up on their hopes and visions for the future. They are bitter souls who become angry and resentful when they see others achieving their goals. Instead of encouraging their fellow humans and finding inspiration in the feats of those who have the zeal and passion to build skill, they try to drag people down to their level. Sometimes they do this by insulting the other person's dream and downplaying their ability, but they also employ another tactic, a more subtle one. Faking concern and worry for the other person's best interest, they encourage the person towards the safer option, the security of status quo. They use fear tactics and the gentle suggestion of failure to keep other people from pursing their goals.

For a long time on my journey towards recovery, I was my own worst troll. I should have left that hospital in the Philippines much earlier but I convinced myself to play it safe by continuing to receive support from Purefoods. When I finally decided that no amount of security was going to stop me from putting myself in the best possible position to learn to walk again, I shut down that negative inner voice and took a risk. I slayed the troll within myself. I forced myself to face my fears and turn my outlook around. The troll within had often reminded me that the doctors had given me a 96% chance of failure. I turned that around and reminded myself that this meant there was a 4% chance of success.

We need to shut down toxic, limiting dialogue in our lives, whether it is with internet trolls, with family members who would project their own worries and fears onto us, or with ourselves. Like all true trailblazers in human society were able to do, we must transcend our limitations by setting our sights far above what the naysayers and doubters believe is possible. We must get our toes out of the water and dive into our lives at the deep end.

Lying there in my hospital bed on a dark night in 2006, I thought about all the dreams that were taken away from me and I was truly bitter. I didn't realize that those didn't have to be my dreams anymore. Instead I could create new and better dreams to pursue. I was once able to bring joy to many people by playing professional basketball and I could still bring joy to people by inspiring them to be all they could be. I could help people on their journey toward making change in their lives. I could speak the truth in love and the truth is simple: nothing in life is ever safe, not even love itself.

If there is one risk that I urge you to take in your life, it would be the risk that comes with loving without limits. Love is exciting; it is adventurous and full of promise. It gives us the ability to transcend the temporal and move with purpose to the attainment of the eternal. Love is leaving our comfort zones, risking everything, and pursuing who we were meant to be all along. Let our first steps out of paralysis be those taken in love.

CHAPTER 11
"FRIENDS IN HIGH PLACES"

In 2011, exactly five years after the accident, I took my wheelchair outside and basked in the glow of a gorgeous midafternoon sun. It was Mother's Day and it seemed hard to imagine that only five years earlier, I had gone through the most painful experience of my life. That Californian Spring day in 2011 was a day to enjoy. The rehabilitation process was paying off. I had developed meaningful relationships with people around me, and I truly felt that my prospects were looking up but I couldn't help think of where I was 58 months prior.

In July of 2006, I was still stuck in a hospital bed in Manila. My hopes and my outlook were dim but what had gotten me through was the support of friends who were not only there for me physically but who were also there to guide me through the many emotions that I was experiencing. These were my true friends—the wheat that remained when the chaff had blown away. Looking back five years on, I realized that I would not have gotten to that point in my recovery without the "first responders" who were there for me when the wounds to my body were at their freshest.

***

Back when I first arrived in the Philippines in 2003, I quickly fell in with a group that came to be known as The Circle. Composed of five members--Jimmy Alapag, Harvey Carey, LJ Moreno, Rich Hardin, and yours truly—The Circle was unbreakable and as tight as any group could be. I met Jimmy, Harvey, and Rich when we were all part of the same PBA draft class. Harvey was selected first out of all of us as the 4th pick of the draft. Jimmy was picked at number 10, I was picked at number 15, and Rich was picked at number 33 to complete the draft-day success for "the Circle." We met LJ Moreno, a beautiful Filipina actress, shortly after that and became five solid friends just trying to make our way through life in Manila, navigating the twists and turns of professional sports and show business. What made our bond truly special was the unconditional support we had for each other.

Jimmy Alapag was, in my mind, the most successful Filipino-American basketball player to ever play in the PBA. He finished his career in the PBA as a 6-time champion, with titles sprinkled from 2003 all the way to 2013. He was an 11-time all-star, as well as the MVP of the league in 2011, his finest season. With his 5'9 and mere 175 pound frame, Jimmy was able to make it on to the list of the 40 greatest PBA players of all time, and he will always be remembered for the clutch three pointer he hit in the 2013 FIBA World Cup qualifier to push the Philippines past rival South Korea and into the 2014 World Cup of Basketball. Despite all this, what stands out to me the most about him was his caring heart.

Before I was injured, Jimmy was there for me. He let me know he had no doubt that I was a star waiting to emerge when I was warming the bench for the Alaska Aces. When I turned things around and starting working my way towards a Most Improved Player award playing for Purefoods, he was there to cheer me on even though he played for a rival team. After the accident, Jimmy was one of the first people at the hospital and he stayed with me regularly until I was ready to fly back to the US. Always humble, Jimmy was the epitome of a leader and he showed his leadership qualities both on and off the basketball court.

Harvey Carey was the highest-picked player among us at number four in the 2003 draft but he played his whole career as if he was a perpetual underdog. He never carried himself as an aloof celebrity, in spite of all his success, and he maintained his down-to-earth personality. He was too focused on raising a family to become involved in the ever-present distractions of Manila. His career numbers reflect his excellence: 7 PBA Championships, an all-star selection in 2011, and 609 career games wherein he consistently averaged north of 6 rebounds a game. Harvey was a double-double machine whose defense propelled his teams to win when it mattered most.

Harvey and I had played together prior to the PBA as we were both from the Bay Area in California. Our bond grew stronger when we broke into the PBA at the same time and we quickly became inseparable. Harvey was the closest thing I had to a confidant, someone whom I could talk to about all my struggles, and I came to rely on his insight in tough spots.

Harvey was there the night I was wheeled into Makati Medical Center and he prayed for me to recover. He backed up those prayers with the unshakable belief that I would one day walk again and spent significant time with me during the PBA off-seasons. I am not sure how far I would have made it without the unwavering support of this gentle giant with a fondness for philosophical discussion. I once said that Harvey was "deeper than the Pacific Ocean," and this was true not only of his musings, but also of the love that he had for me.

Rich was the last of our group to be picked and, while he did not have the same career as Jimmy or Harvey, he later went on to successful ventures as a personal trainer and conditioning coach. He spent countless hours with me at the hospital when I was hurt and kept a steadfast belief in my ability to recover.

The Circle would not have been complete without LJ Moreno. LJ had made it big in the Philippine world of showbusiness as an actress. Moreno was her screen name and she was born Lari Jeanne Ricafort. LJ was the sister in our group and she brought a much-needed feminine energy and perspective to the Circle. LJ and Jimmy were the "Monica and Chandler" of our group and eventually married in 2010. Before the accident, when those of us in The Circle were kicking around Manila, I appreciated how LJ took care of us and made us feel we were part of her family.

LJ basically adopted us and showed us how to carry ourselves and thrive in the unfamiliar world of the Manila limelight. She gave us encouragement and connected us to key people in Philippine society. All our careers might have ended differently without the influence and unconditional support LJ provided. She brought that same encouragement and nurturing outlook to the hospital after I was injured and was a great source of comfort to me.

Not exactly part of the Circle but important to me and my recovery none the less was Nats Calinawan. I met Nats shortly after I was drafted to the Aces. He was a friend of a friend at first, the General Manager of a restaurant many of the team members visited after games. He quickly became my friend too and when I was injured, he went above and beyond what any regular friend would do. Nats was at the hospital almost every single day and he was my family during the toughest period of my life. From making Jell-O for me to bringing me dinner every night when I was finally able to eat solid food, Nats was a model of consistency and steadfast love.

Nats fed me when I couldn't lift the fork to my own mouth. He stayed late into the night at the hospital because he felt that I needed the company. I cried out to him when I was frustrated and he never said a word. He was always the listening ear and he became a trusted confidant because of his steady presence.

To this day, I can't explain what drove Nats to give up significant bits of his life to be there for me at the hospital. I never asked him to do any of the things he did but he performed all those acts of kindness with joy and a profound sense of passion. Because of Nats I know there are people out there who will stand by you in your worst moments. His everyday small acts of kindness made him a hero in my life.

And last but not least, there was Rob Duat, another great friend during this time and a Filipino-American basketball player who literally paved the way for guys like me. He was a few years older than I was but had attended the same college and high school in the US a few years ahead of me and was a bit of Hometown Hero. I wanted to emulate Rob in more ways than one. He too had started out slow in his career with the PBA but went on to win the Most Improved Player award in 2002, a testament to his grit and determination.

Rob was like a big brother to me and one of the first things he did when he found out I was paralyzed was to inspire me to achieve a new goal. Once he knew I would no longer be able to lace up my basketball sneakers, he began to encourage me to aim to be a pro at my new calling in life. It really helped that Rob and I went back to the same city once he retired and I decided to return to the US to rehab.

It was tough for Rob to adjust back to "normal" life in Hayward. He missed the limelight in Manila but used his struggle to once again inspire me and guide me through my own challenges. Both of us missed the big leagues but Rob knew that there was more to me than just being a basketball player. To this day, I am thankful for the impact he had on my life. Now I try to be like Rob because he has been a pillar of strength for many people in his life. I was fortunate enough to be able to rely on that strength when I had almost none of my own. Rob and these other men all inspired me to reflect on the concept of friendship and what Jesus saw one day in Capernaum according to a Biblical account.

> *"A few days later, when Jesus again entered Capernaum, the people heard that he had come home. They gathered in such large numbers that there was no room left, not even outside the door, and he preached the word to them. Some men came, bringing to him a paralyzed man, carried by four of them. Since they could not get him to Jesus because of the crowd, they made an opening in the roof above Jesus by digging through it and then lowered the mat the man was lying on. When Jesus saw their faith, he said to the paralyzed man, 'Son, your sins are forgiven.*[14]*"*
>
> -Mark 2:1-2:2

***

As late as the year 2001, a Gallup poll showed that Americans averaged about nine "close friends, not including family and relatives[15]." This was before the time of social media, when people merely used cellular phones to call each other. In this Gallup poll, Americans were depicted as mostly satisfied with their relationships and felt they had a solid number of people they could rely on when things went sideways.

Fast forward to the year 2018. A study from health insurer Cigna found that most Americans now reported feeling "lonely, left out and

---

[14] Mark 2:1-2:12, *The Holy Bible: New International Version, NIV.* (Biblical Inc. 1973, 1978, 1984, 2011).

[15] News.gallup.com/poll/10891

not known.[16]" In that study, the identified number of "close friends" that the Gallup poll identified in 2001 as nine, dropped to between two and five. The study further elaborated that one out of five adults regularly felt lonely. Similar articles and studies have emerged over the last five years with similar conclusions; in spite of us bragging about our 1,000 to 5,000 friends on Facebook, human beings are generally more isolated and lack the kind of meaningful interactions with others that they had 18 years ago.

Prior to getting hurt, I thought that I had thousands of friends. I was a celebrity in a country that celebrated basketball players like Japan celebrates Sumo wrestlers. Everywhere I went, I got special treatment. People approached me like I was a walking good luck charm that they just had to get close to. They wanted to hang out with me and I took this to mean that I had a great many friends. I didn't notice, or maybe I didn't care, that these people barely knew me and I barely knew them. They were acquaintances for the most part, fair-weather friends at best. They hung with me through the good times but, once I got hurt and they could no longer benefit from their association with me, they quickly scattered.

This scattering or dwindling by my thousands of so-called "friends" was in stark contrast to efforts my inner circle made to be there for me when I needed them most. From the night I was paralyzed, my inner circle made a consolidated effort to keep me afloat. Losing the ability to move any part of your body from the neck down is like drowning in a pool. It's exhausting just trying to keep your head above water and, for a long time, I felt like I wanted to give up. I wanted to be free from the pain—a kind of pain unlike anything I had ever experienced prior to that point in my life.

In the midst of my struggles, when I felt most alone, it was my close circle of friends that kept me from sinking. They didn't allow me to give up and drown. They hauled me out from beneath the weight of my sorrow and despair and raised me up. As with that group of men in Capernaum, it took collaboration to bring me to the roof, to make a hole, and to lower me to the feet of our Savior.

***

---

[16] www.barna.com, "US Adults Have Few Friends—and They're Mostly Alike," October 23, 2018.

Aside from the help of "the Circle," there was another group of friends who rallied around me to help me prepare for my rehabilitation in the US and I would be remiss if I did not mention them. My dream of walking again was an expensive one and leaving the Philippines to enroll in the SCI-FIT program in California was going to be an incredible drain on my resources. Key people stepped up to the plate and threw a fund-raising event for me as a sort of "going away present."

Sarah Meier, a local celebrity and model, used her connections to gather people's support for the event. Chiqui, the wife of former player Jeff Flowers, used her family's connections to secure important venues and player presence. Tying the efforts together was LJ, my constant supporter and sister, who increased the magnitude of the event by virtue of her influence and the positive energy she projected. The trio organized a celebrity exhibition basketball game to be played by some of the country's top players along with more than a few retired legends of Philippine basketball. The event also featured a halftime show for the ages with Hip-Hop and Street dancers performing to amp the crowd.

At this point in time--September 2006--I had already returned to the US to begin my rehab at SCI-FIT. I was living in California again, away from the limelight in Manila and it would have been easy for everyone to forget about me. It was, therefore, a very touching gesture to see those three women organize this event which was officially called: "Step by Step: The Eugene Tejada Fundraiser." The event culminated in an after party at Fiamma bar in downtown Makati with a special auction of sports memorabilia donated by some of the country's biggest hoops legends. Some of the featured items in the auction were an autographed Elton Brand LA Clippers jersey along with a signed Houston Rockets jersey from no less than Tracy McGrady, which Adidas generously donated as an auction item for my fundraiser.

When the dust settled, the fundraiser had brought in about 20,000 US Dollars to help me in my rehabilitation. While this money was used up after only a few months at SCI-FIT, I sincerely believe that the fundraiser played a key role in my being able to walk again. I knew that rehab was going to be expensive, but thanks to the efforts of the people behind the Step by Step Fundraiser, I was able to get within striking distance of my goal. The momentum and goodwill they built up for me propelled me forward and I would not have gotten this far without their help.

***

The support of close friends didn't end when I flew back to the United States as a paralytic. I had a band of brothers waiting for me there who were willing and ready to join me in the trenches. I call them the Jerk Crew and they were an important part of my healing and recovery. They stood by me, day in and day out, as I went through rehab, keeping me company and enduring my many mood swings and not-so-positive outpourings of emotion as I struggled to come to terms with my paralysis.

The Jerk Crew, comprised of five selfless men, did a lot of the dirty work that never seems to get praised in stories like mine. They took me out when I didn't feel like it. They built ramps for me and carried me up flights of stairs just so we could enjoy each other's company. They opened up their homes and their families so that I could heal in the context of a loving community. They are John Alacantara, JR Marasigan, Edmer Soto, Romel Aduviso, and Kris Birco.

Each of these men brought pieces of themselves into the fight to make me whole again and contributed greatly towards my recovery. John Alacantara, one of my heroes growing up and the person who first gave me serious exposure to the game of basketball, was my next-door neighbor in Hayward. He had a legitimate basketball court in his backyard when we were growing up and it was at that court that I learned to play. John helped me develop my basketball skills as a kid and I leaned on him again to guide me towards a new field of development.

I first met JR Marasigan while working as a waiter prior to leaving for the Philippines in 2003. JR happened to be in the Philippines at the time of the accident and he went to find me at the Makati Medical Center as soon as he heard the news. He saw firsthand how serious my injury was and provided the rest of the Jerk Crew with frequent updates. JR was also the handyman of the group. He could build anything and he put his talents to use building me my own disability ramp that allowed me to roll in and out of my parents' house. He modified equipment for me and never charged me for any of the services he provided. I am thankful for his creativity and ingenuity and the way he used them to help me find ways to rise above my limitations.

If John was my shoulder to lean on and JR was a set of helping hands, then Edmer Soto was a pair of listening ears. Edmer and I met during my college days when we worked retail together. A warm soul with a vibrant personality, he was always trying to make people smile and laugh. Edmer was a Christian who lived out his faith by being of service to people like me. He encouraged me when I was down by reading Bible passages. The conversations I would have with him were very meaningful and he made it a point that we met regularly every week during my recovery. Edmer reminded me of God's promises for my life and how I was meant to overcome in spite of all the adversity that I had faced thus far. It was during my talks with him that I began to understand how my life had a purpose and that the accident was a way for me to fulfill my true destiny.

Rommel Aduviso, the beating heart of the group, provided empathy when I needed it most. If I was hurting, so was he. Always tuned into what I was going through, Rommel showed me love and loyalty by consistently dropping what he was doing just to be with me. His sincerity and friendship helped me heal and inspired me to look beyond my injury and be empathetic towards those who had gone through their own tragedies and personal setbacks the way Rommel had with me. Years later, Rommel would be the best man at my wedding but, in the early days of my recovery, he personified the kind of selfless sacrifice that the Bible talks about when describing how a real friend should act.

Rounding out the Jerk Crew was Kris Birco. Kris was like blood to me. Our mothers grew up together in Philippines and we called each other cousins even if we weren't officially related. Kris was the person who gathered everyone together much like Vin Diesel's character in the first Fast and the Furious movie. He planned barbecues and meals and these gathering helped me feel normal again. By doing this, Kris helped give me exactly what I needed—the ability to heal in the context of a community that loved me unconditionally. I still had much pain and adversity to overcome but being together with the boys gave me hope and inspired me to keep going on my tough road towards eventually standing up and walking again.

***

People say you can't choose your family or your siblings but you can always cultivate your relationship with them to the point that you'd choose them if given the chance. This is how I feel about my sister Dana and my brother James. If God were to have given me a choice to have any two siblings in the world, I would have chosen both of them many times over.

Mother's Day of 2006 was a tragic day for me but it began as a happy one. Dana had graduated from college a few hours before the game but, once she heard what had happened to me, she booked the first flight she could to Manila from California. Rushing to be at my side, she arrived in Manila exhausted from the hours of travel but determined to be by my side.

Dana stayed by my side in the hospital and cheered my progress no matter how negative the doctors' reports became. When she heard that I had only a 4% chance of ever walking again, she reminded me that 4% is still something and encouraged me to give it my all, in spite of the odds. Eventually she had to leave to return to California but even her departure worked out for the best. God was sending her ahead of me and, when I eventually came back to the US for rehabilitation, she was waiting at the airport to greet me and to make me feel at home again. Dana was my rock while I was recovering. She drove me to physical therapy sessions after I was discharged from the hospital and she cared for me at home. To this day, I cannot even begin to comprehend the sacrifices she made for me.

My brother James has always been my biggest fan. Technically, I was the younger brother but I always felt like I had to be the "big" brother when we were growing up because James had a learning disability. I was physically stronger and looked out for him, keeping him from being bullied. After I got hurt, James and I reversed roles. He had to step into the role of big brother as my paralysis forced me to rely heavily on him. James rose to the challenge and was there for me although it can't have been easy for him. He got the short end of the stick when I was in the middle of an emotional meltdown or bout of depression. I regularly lost my temper over the smallest thing but James remained calm and steady. He showed his love in a quiet but powerful and patient way.

***

In the book *Stillness Is the Key*[17], Ryan Holiday says, "a good relationship requires us to be virtuous, present, empathetic, generous, open, and willing to be part of a larger whole." I thought about the friends in my life who were all these things to me. I could not have gotten well without the small sustaining acts of kindness that they showed me; my recovery would have stalled.

I needed the friend who would go out and buy me food when I could not walk to the nearest restaurant. I needed the sibling who would faithfully drive me to and from physical therapy sessions. I needed the childhood buddy to build me a wheelchair ramp. All these actions added up to an environment of healing, and I was able to become whole as a result of my friends' cumulative sacrifices.

Sigmund Freud once said that "love is the greatest educator. We learn when we give it. We learn when we get it." Through the constant giving and receiving of love from those valuable people in my life, I was able to buck the odds and turn that 4% chance that the doctors gave me into a sure thing. The commitment, time, and unwavering support that my community poured into me were the ingredients needed for my recipe of recovery. The end result was a changed life and I am forever grateful for the love and support of my friends.

The Bible says, in John 15:13, that "Greater love has no one than this: to lay down one's life for one's friends." Even if my friends never literally stepped in front of a bullet for me, their acts of service and kindness were a sacrifice and an offering of their lives. They loved me the way Jesus asked us to love each other, unconditionally and ever-presently, and through this love, they brought me closer to God's healing touch.

---

[17] Ryan Holiday, *Stillness is the Key*. Portfolio Books, 2019.

CHAPTER 12
"THE FOUR WORDS"

In 2016, ten years after the accident, the world was very different for me. I had made significant progress in both my physical and emotional rehabilitation but there were still some things that were holding me back. Living in the US had been a welcome break from the limelight and it had done me a lot of good just to be a normal guy. Heaven knows that it was beneficial to be able to recuperate away from the media and everyone else who saw me as an entertainer or as a celebrity rather than as a human being.

My life in a wheelchair may not have been as exciting as life as a professional basketball player but it was deep, contemplative, and I had time to reflect on my next mission. Having reached my initial goals of being able to walk and able to drive again, I thought about the next phase of my development. I began to consider the inner conflicts of my mind and how I could resolve them.

***

> *A Cherokee elder was teaching his young grandson about life. "A fight is going on inside me," he said to the boy. "It is a terrible fight between two wolves. One wolf is evil—he is anger, envy, sorrow, regret, greed, arrogance, self-pity, guilt, resentment, lies, false pride, superiority, and self-doubt. The other is good—he is joy, peace, love, hope, serenity, humility,*

> *kindness, generosity, truth, compassion and faith. This same fight is going on inside you and inside every other person, too."*
> *The boy thought about it for a minute then asked his grandfather, "Which wolf will win?" The elder replied:*
> *"The one YOU FEED."*
>
> -Traditional Tsalagi Tale

Overcoming my inner struggles was not instant. I achieved peace within myself in 2016 but in a gradual and methodical manner. Throughout my whole ordeal with my paralysis and subsequent recovery, I had to learn to avoid using four very specific words: Can't, Need, Bad, and Try. These words sound simple enough yet their influence is profound. The way we use them in both our outer and inner monologue can subtly influence our quality of life. They are words that I consistently try to take out of my vocabulary because they limit the way I am able to experience the world.

Word 1: Can't

The word *can't* is a contraction for the longer, more formal *cannot*. Can't is quick and casual. Cannot is imposing and a speaker uses it with purpose. I believe that the contracted form of the word has somehow desensitized us to its destructive power. We throw it out there quickly and often and accept the self-imposed limitations the word places on us.

Initially, when I was paralyzed, the doctors said that I *can't* realistically look forward to a normal life. I *can't* hope to walk again. Fourteen years after the accident that changed my life, other peoples' *can'ts* had become my accomplishments. If I had accepted the limitations they tried to place on me, I would not have opened myself up to the possibility of finding my true love and becoming a father. I would have allowed their negativity--however well-meaning--to build a ceiling over my growth and development.

Every day, billions of people dream of something better for themselves but they make themselves prisoner of this all too powerful word: *can't*. With this in mind, I urge you to rid yourself of the thought that there is anything you cannot accomplish. If your desire is to be a better dad to your children, do not place any limitations on that desire. Find ways to ask "how can I be better" instead of sinking into defeatist thinking that makes you declare, "I'd really like to be a better father but I just *can't* seem to balance the time between work and home life." The word can't is a manifestation of a limiting belief that seeks to rob us of our true potential.

Often, people in my life tell me, "You know, Gene, I'd really like to change but old habits die hard." That might be true. Old habits may die hard but the fact is that they can and do die. If there is something that we want to change in our lives, the word "can't" must be removed from our lexicon. Begin asking the right questions, the ones that make it impossible to answer with a negative like *can't*. For example, ask "how can I change?" instead of "can I truly change." By steering ourselves away from this word, our lives will become open canvases of possibility and direction. We will begin to see all the bright hues of the masterpiece that God has designed in us.

Word 2: Need

We live in a society that is not only geared towards the fulfillment of needs but towards the creation of needs. We are always in need of something and if, even for a moment we aren't, an advertiser will come along and tell us that we are. So, let's play a game of "What If?" What if I learned to discount my own desires and learned to be content with what I had? What if I learned to prioritize the people around me instead of being so focused on my own necessities? I believe that by eliminating the word "need" from our vocabulary, we immediately become more grateful for everything that we have in the present moment.

We might never be able to eliminate the use of the word entirely, but let us at least eliminate using it as a verb and in such a broad context: "I need to have that promotion." "I need to have that pair of shoes." "I need this right now!" If we narrow the scope of the word's meaning to "a thing that is required for survival," we reserve it for the most crucial elements in life: air, water, food, love. We can all but remove its casual usage from our lives, allowing us to be a little less self-centered and focused on all that we lack.

One of the things that helped me move beyond obsessively focusing on what I had lost during my time in the hospital was thinking of other people. Instead of allowing myself to spiral into depression over the fact that I *needed* to be playing basketball again and I *needed* to be earning money, I started to think of how I could inspire others with my story. I changed my focus from my own needs to what I thought I could do to help others meet their needs. I found purpose in this and one can never be too depressed when one has a purpose.

Over the years, I have been able to use my story to bring hope to quadriplegics and people who have been afflicted with the same issues that I suffered from. I feel a sense of fulfillment every time I am able to inspire a fellow human being to begin the process towards being whole again: mentally, emotionally, physically, and spiritually whole. It has taken time but I have learned to let go of the concept that achievement is the result of the fulfillment of personal needs. Achievement is not limited to material things.

By learning to look outside my own circle of need, I was able to see that there has always been something greater at work. There is a kingdom being built around us by our actions and our interactions. This is God's kingdom as it is reflected here on earth. My most selfish drives and achievements built me an earthly kingdom in which I was adored and had everything I thought I needed but that kingdom was a fragile thing. Only after it crumbled and the dust settled was I finally able to find self-actualization. I was no longer just in it for me; I was in it to serve others and to make sure that other people wouldn't have to go through the process of recovering from physical paralysis alone. I was a part of something larger and more important. I was helping to build a kingdom that will last.

Word 3: Bad

Good. Bad. Thumbs up. Thumbs down. Upvote. Down vote. Like. Dislike.

Life is a system of ratings and we have all become critics and judges. We get so caught up in our own stories that sometimes people have to assume the role of villain in the narratives we tell ourselves just so we know which box to put them in. We are quick to judge when people violate even the smallest social norm. But just like in the show *Cobra Kai*, we find that things are not always what they seem and the bad guy often has his own backstory that we are not aware of.

I have eliminated the word *bad* from my vocabulary and have seen wonders because of it. I've already told you about Mick, the man who ended my career, who was tormented by what happened for years. I have shared the story of the woman who broke my heart by leaving me when I supposedly needed (there's that word again) her the most. I wanted to characterize both these people as *bad*. It would have been very easy to do so. One broke my body and the other broke my heart but by categorizing people and events as bad, we fail to account for the fact that problems are just opportunities in disguise. We fail to understand that things which seem negative at first can turn out to have the most profoundly positive effects in our lives.

My co-author of this book shared a story with me of a friend with whom he went to high school. That friend ended up working at the World Trade Center in New York shortly after graduating from college. On the morning of September 11, 2001, Jesse (not his real name) woke up with a very *bad* stomach flu. He was vomiting all morning and had to call in sick. Looking back at it, wasn't that the best case of the stomach flu he ever had? It literally saved his life! There are hundreds and thousands of other occurrences and events that show up in our lives looking like curses but are really blessings in disguise. Get rid of the negative lenses that you view those events with and put on a pair of rose-colored glasses. For all you know, the *bad* instances in your life were really the best things that ever happened to you even if you never got to see the obvious reasons why and the direct correlation like Jesse did.

Word 4: Try

How often have we heard or made the excuse "I'll try to be there?" I believe it was Yoda who said, in his inimitable fashion, "try not! Do or do not. There is no try." Either we will do something or we won't do something. Try is a cop out, a supposedly polite way of implying "no" when we can't quite bring ourselves to say no. No can be the hardest word in the English language at times: we struggle to tell ourselves no and we struggle to say it to others. We are afraid of offending or being seen in a negative light. So instead we vacillate and prevaricate and give flaky answers so we don't have to be honest. This doesn't do anyone any favors. It leaves everyone in a place of ambiguity and makes it impossible to plan properly. So as the old saying goes: "Just Say No!"

Matthew 5:37 is very clear on this matter: *"Let what you say be simply 'Yes, I will' or 'No, I won't.' Anything beyond this is from the evil one."* Those who say they will *try* to get better at something are communicating to you implicitly that they really won't. They are setting themselves up for failure at the onset because of the language that they are using. So why do we keep saying we will try?

The next time we are faced with a challenge, let's face it by saying "Yes, I will." This removes that tiny level of doubt that allows us to subconsciously self-sabotage our best efforts from the very beginning. When we commit to something, let us leave no room to back out. Otherwise, let's be honest and say "No. I really will not do it" and save time and energy. Notice that I said *will not* instead of *cannot*, implying choice and not ability. We make choices in our lives that are often weightier than we realize. We may believe that we are giving something an honest attempt but by beginning the endeavor with *try* in mind we have already conceded to the possibility of failure. Say instead, "I will do it until I do it right." By eliminating the word try from our vocabulary, we do not allow ourselves to take the coward's way out!

***

By gradually eliminating these four words from my life, I was able to take a giant leap forward. I no longer felt like an impostor playing a part that was really about someone else. I no longer felt the *need* to please other people. I no longer told myself that that I *can't* be the person I truly desire to be. I had a blank canvas in front of me on which to paint my own self-portrait and I had eliminated an unhealthy spirit of competition left over from my basketball days in which I believed that life was a win-lose proposition, that someone had to suffer a loss in order for another to take the victory. The reality is there is more than enough for all of us to share in this world.

As I opened my eyes to the kindness of those around me, I realized that most of the people in my life wanted to cooperate with me rather than compete against me. These positive influences moved me away from *trying* to better than the next person and, instead, allowed me to be happy that both of us were being lifted up by a common experience. The next time you are tempted to feel bitter because a colleague got a promotion instead of you, I suggest that you celebrate with them instead. Who knows, maybe their promotion is the start of a wave of good things for the people in your circle. Or, for all you know, it is a sign from God that you were meant to do something radically different and immensely more satisfying.

I stopped looking at my accident as a *bad* thing. A friend of mine once asked me, in the style of Morpheus from the popular movie *The Matrix*, "if you could take a magic pill that would turn back time, allow you to prevent the accident, and have another 10 years playing professional basketball, would you take the pill?" The only catch, he said, was that I would be the same person I was before the accident. I wouldn't have acquired all the knowledge and self-awareness that came with my injury and subsequent recovery.

I thought about the question deeply and I replied, "No. I'd rather be in a wheelchair." Despite all the trauma and pain, there were liberating aspects to what happened to me. I had been locked inside myself and given the opportunity to get to know the two wolves that fought within me—the good wolf and the bad wolf. When I finally began to free myself from my physical constraints and regain a normal life it was with the understanding that I would move forward with the good wolf at my side and let the other starve.

CHAPTER 13

"FACETS OF FORGIVENESS"

In 2018 I sat down and reflected back on the twelve years that had passed since my accident. Twelve years. A dozen. More than a decade. A lot of things in my life had changed. For one, I was able to reconnect with the love of my life. After praying about our relationship, we got married and became the parents of two wonderful twin boys. I had a career as an Uber driver—all that time spent learning to drive again was paying off—though I still often thought about how my career and my life would have played out if I had not gotten hurt.

Most likely, I would have played professional basketball for another 10 years or so, retiring in 2016 or 2017. That's about the time that my friends Jimmy and Harvey chose to hang up their sneakers for good. I probably would have been a totally different person at the end of those ten years. My life in Manila would have stayed much the same though I would have been earning more as my career progressed. I would have had more money but probably not a whole lot more perspective.

I thought about these things in September of 2018 and felt, perhaps surprisingly, a little frustrated about how my life had not moved forward as far as I would have liked it to. Sure, I had emotional breakthroughs and triumphs and gained a greater understanding of myself. I had bucked the odds and had regained the ability to do many of the things I had been told I would never be able to do. I was walking with the aid of walking sticks and I was able to drive a car competently enough to be a highly rated Uber driver. However, a part of me still felt incomplete. I began to sense that, even with all I had accomplished, God had something more for me in store.

It was at this time that God began to speak to me in a series of visions as I slept. Nights in September 2018 were not easy for me. I was afraid to go to sleep at times because I knew I would experience the same vision I'd had the night before, and the night before that. The visions were all about me and how the Lord wanted to peel back the various layers of my life and expose my core. The visions were raw and unsettling and left me feeling exposed in ways that I didn't want to be. I was mostly recovered physically at this point but there was clearly still something missing in my life from a spiritual aspect and God was going to get the message across to me so that I could finally break-through in the way that He intended.

***

> *"Therefore, the kingdom of heaven is like a king who wanted to settle accounts with his servants. As he began the settlement, a man who owed him ten thousand bags of gold was brought to him. Since he was not able to pay, the master ordered that he and his wife and his children and all that he had be sold to repay the debt. At this the servant fell on his knees before him. 'Be patient with me,' he begged, 'and I will pay back everything.' The servant's master took pity on him, canceled the debt and let him go. But when that servant went out, he found one of his fellow servants who owed him a hundred silver coins. He grabbed him and began to choke him. 'Pay back what you owe me!' he demanded. His fellow servant fell to his knees and begged him, 'Be patient with me, and I will pay it back.' But he refused. Instead, he went off and had the man thrown into prison until he could pay the debt. When the other servants saw what had happened, they were outraged and went and told their master everything that had happened. Then the master called the servant in. 'You wicked servant,' he said. 'I canceled all that debt of yours because you begged me to. Shouldn't you have had mercy on your fellow servant just as I had on you?' In anger his master*

handed him over to the jailers to be tortured, until he should pay back all he owed."[18]

-Matthew 18:23-18:24

I thought about this passage from the Book of Matthew in the days following that series of visions from God. The Lord impressed upon my heart that I needed to fix an aspect of my life that was holding me back and this passage was the perfect illustration. I believe that Jesus used this analogy, the concept of being unable to repay a debt we owe, to illustrate just how many facets forgiveness has.

Part of the problem with society is that we expect justice when we are offended but we expect mercy when we are the offending party. The parable above of the servant who was shown mercy and forgiveness by his master but could not show mercy in return and demanded restitution is a perfect illustration of the "default" setting of our flawed human nature. Before I was paralyzed, I looked down in contempt upon those who had disabilities or deformities. I subconsciously believed that they were somehow less significant than someone able bodied and felt that they used their condition as an excuse to get other people to feel sorry for them. I suppose it is all fear of the unknown. I didn't know at the time what it was like to be disabled and to imagine what it was like was too uncomfortable. I didn't want to think what life would be like in a wheelchair. Once I was in a wheelchair, however, and the shoe was on the other foot, I assumed a large percentage of the population felt the same way about me and then it seemed highly unfair.

Decent society generally accepts that deriding a person who is physically disabled is utterly ridiculous and narrow-minded. Likewise, looking down on someone who is mentally handicapped or facing psychological issues is cruel and bigoted. Casting judgement and criticizing people's spiritual handicaps, on the other hand, has become entertainment. When a man is caught having an affair and hurts his wife and family, we are so quick to smirk and make the familiar "tsk, tsk" sound. We gossip and gab about it; "He sure was caught with his pants down!" We pat ourselves on the

---

[18] Matthew 18:23-18:24, *The Holy Bible, New International Version, NIV.* (Biblica Inc. 1973, 1978, 1984, 2011)

back and say, "I am so glad that I'm smart enough not to fall into that person's sin."

We feel good about ourselves when we witness someone else's spiritual shortcoming because we believe we are superior to them. We may pretend that we want to know more details about the scandal so we can help that person but, the truth is, that person's sin makes us feel better because our own uncleanness suddenly doesn't look so bad. We want to point and say, "look, he owes the master 10,000 bags of gold! Why, I only owe the master 5,000 bags of gold! See how much better I am!"

What a ridiculous conceit! Can you imagine if we made those types of comparisons to people who were not as physically or mentally able as we are? While it may be difficult to admit this to ourselves, we fall into the trap of judging others and we may even want drama to happen to other people so we can feel better about how "normal" our own lives are by comparison. This is why *Us Weekly* and other gossip publications make so much money in an age where print media is supposed to be going extinct. If we are not happy, it is easier to look for people who are worse off than we are and use that to assuage our own angst rather than work on ways for us to better ourselves and our own lives.

***

The point of the parable of the wicked servant who owed his master money is that forgiveness should not exist as a one-way street but as a principle that guides all human relationships and that we pay forward to those in need. Think about this the next time someone cuts you off on the freeway or you receive bad service at a business establishment and you feel your blood pressure rising and anger begins to blur your vision.

About the time that I was having those visions, a woman from Georgia was accused of firing a gun at a McDonalds because she was served cold French fries. Now, before you judge her like we are all prone to do, let's think about how many times we have allowed rage to overpower our better instincts and nobler spirits when we didn't get our way. How many times have we lost our cool when someone behaved in a manner that we deemed unreasonable? If we are to be at peace and in tune with the Spirit of God, we must act like servants whose debts have recently been canceled and be willing to cancel the debts of others.

Being able to forgive means having a healthy view of ourselves and a realistic opinion of our own sinfulness. We should not buy into the popular train of thought that we can conform everything to suit our desires and invent our own morality. We must have a sober view of who we really are. The fact is, we are all sinners who have been forgiven of a debt so great we would not even know how to begin to repay it. By accepting this, we can own a type of self-confidence that comes from being secure in our relationship with God and allows us to find the grace and strength to forgive the sinners around us.

What does it mean to walk in this kind of liberation? It means that we can finally throw off the yoke created by the debt of our sin and receive God's forgiveness openly and fully. Without this weight we can rise up with joy in our hearts and a new spring in our step and know that we are the lucky ones. Someone paid the penalty for our sins and the ledger has been wiped clean. We do not need to repay the 10,000 bags of gold we owe the Master. He forgave us, not because we deserved it, but because He is merciful.

The kind of people who will change the world are not those who are blindly positive and only able to see the good in life. People who will change the world are those who are negative enough to know that they are absolutely broken. They are willing see the darkness and do not turn away pretending it doesn't exist. They decide instead to accept it as something to be overcome and forgiven and are thereby liberated from its power.

Once we figure out that we are screw-ups but screw-ups that have been forgiven, we can go out into the world and extend grace and mercy to the most insufferable of humans. Just imagine how amazing the world would be if people offered words of blessing to one another instead of flipping each other off when they are cut off in their driving lanes. This is not a theology of purely positive thinking. Rather, it is the theology of reality and it involves keeping a sober view of ourselves so that we act like people humbled by the fact that we have recently been pardoned of a great debt.

***

Having an appropriate and accurate view of self means being able to move on from our own mistakes. We cannot occupy both ends of the spectrum and be both martyrs and oppressors. We end up becoming the guy who chokes his fellow servant for 100 silver coins and then tears his clothes and flings himself into the dirt crying, "I don't even deserve to live." While this is certainly a normal initial reaction to our transgressions, it must not become a perpetual state of being. The truth is, complete forgiveness requires that we also forgive ourselves and move on from past mistakes. The Lord showed me that this was one of the main areas in my life that I had to fix in order to take that next leap forward. I needed to be able to forgive myself and enjoy being in the Lord's presence as His forgiven son.

Let us imagine the parable of the forgiven servant from the Master's perspective and picture him watching his servant go out and extend mercy to his fellow servants, forgiving them their debts as well. Think of the pleasure he would feel to witness the peace and joy he instigated within his household. It would be like a parent watching their child opening their presents on Christmas morning.

The Master wouldn't want us to wallow in self-pity. God does not want us to be like a sorrowful Homer Simpson who said to his wife, in one of the best episodes of *The Simpsons* ever, "No, don't serve me any breakfast. I don't deserve it."[19] The television episode is humorous in that it features a very large, grown man acting like a sulking child and refusing sustenance because of his guilt. God doesn't want us to sulk or wallow. Instead, He wants us to take a healthy view of ourselves and move forward with our lives with the opportunity to do better. Our debt has been repaid and we should be imagining life as an experience full of endless possibilities.

The person who does not forgive themselves and chooses to wallow in their guilt quickly becomes self-pitying. That self-pity will then inevitably grow into bitterness and resentment. The false-martyr goes out into the world full of rage and bitterness. They resent themselves and they take out their frustration on the world.

People who live with a 360-degree view of forgiveness are able to forgive themselves and others. They are not arrogant because they know that their status as "debt free" does not come from their own hard work. It flows from the mercy of a great and loving Savior, one who bled and died for others to be pardoned of their transgressions. Because they are forgiven by their Master, they are able to live a life of excitement and profound joy. Yes, problems may come and they may encounter pain and hardships, but

---

[19] *The Simpsons*, Matt Groening. 20th Century Fox, 1989.

no matter how many earthly bills might stack up, they can always look at their lives and know that the greatest of their debts has been paid.

We must expand our limited views of forgiveness. Forgiveness has many facets and complexities. It does not mean you have to be a doormat and let others abuse your kindness. What it means is that we can act from a spirit of gratefulness in the knowledge that we are pardoned. God took the post-dated check we wrote him and he tore that thing up! He said, "No longer am I holding this over you. Now come and abide in Me!" This is the most wonderful aspect of forgiveness. Because the Master has forgiven us, we don't have to be so hard on ourselves or on others!

***

In the weeks that followed my series of visions, I noticed large breakthroughs happening in my life. I no longer felt like an impostor trying to be someone I was not. I emerged as a man victorious, someone who was able to truly abide in the love of His Savior. I rid myself of any sort of regret about what happened in the past. I stopped fretting about the money I missed out on in professional basketball. I stopped thinking about what could have been. I started focusing on what lay ahead of me. I began to understand that both my paralysis and subsequent recovery were ordained by God so that others could be inspired by my struggles and I knew that the message, in the end, was going to be about Him. I forgave myself and I forgave others.

Forgiveness is not something that comes easily but if we truly think about it, the opposite of forgiveness—building resentment inside and letting toxic rage consume us quietly—is a much more costly endeavor in the long run. If we are able to let go of all the things that happened in the past, we will be more prepared to receive the blessings of our future and become part of the wonderful destiny that awaits all people who know what true freedom is.

CHAPTER 14
"A LOVER'S KISS"

The year was 2019 and it had been roughly thirteen years since the accident. I looked back at some of the near misses that I had—like almost dying riding in the back of that ambulance because I was choking on my own vomit—and I saw how far I had come from a time when I celebrated simply being able to move my right big toe. So many people had been there to minister to me during those thirteen years; I had received blessings, well-wishes, and aid from hundreds of amazing people but of all of the people who blessed me during this time there was one person who stood out far above the rest.

***

I first met Andrea, the woman who would eventually become my wife, during my party days in the Philippines, back in the year 2004, two years before I was paralyzed in that fateful game. When I first met her, I was very young and I was enjoying life in the only way I knew how. I was still optimistic that my fortunes with the Alaska Aces would change—that Coach Cone would finally open up some playing time for me—but I wasn't really putting in the work required for that to happen. The one area where I was putting in time and effort was in the Manila social scene where I made sure I was intimately familiar with every happening bar in the city.

One night, while I was making my usual rounds at the nightclubs, a half-German/half-Filipina girl caught my eye and I was instantly intrigued. She seemed different from the other woman I had dated and I just knew that I had to talk to her. I approached her and introduced myself. She told me her name was Andrea and that she had seen me around a couple of nights earlier and had noticed me then. She and I connected right away. I found out we were both from California; she was from Long Beach and I was from Hayward. She had just graduated from the University of Southern California and was vacationing in the Philippines for the summer. That first warm Manila night when we met, I knew there was something special about her.

Andrea and I went on several dates before she returned to the US. One of our earliest dates stands out because it was nearly disastrous and might have ended things before they began. I was incredibly excited to meet up with Andrea that particular night and my hopes were riding high. We had agreed to meet at a certain place for me to pick her up and I was to call her when I got there but when I tried her number, it was disconnected. Convinced that she had "ghosted" me, I tried to pull up my big boy pants and convince myself that I didn't care all that much. I was about to head home with my tail between my legs when I realized that I had been texting a woman named Amanda by mistake. Andrea had not, in fact, rejected me.

Now this story might seem stupid to you and I completely understand if it does. I'd love to say this was a once off thing but this sort of behavior was pretty much par for the course during this not-so-bright part of my life. I tried to compensate for all my insecurities by getting with as many women as possible, so much so that keeping track of their names was tricky at times. I wasn't in a place where I had enough self-awareness to realize that the right woman was standing in front of me, waiting for me to be a better man.

After realizing my mistake, I called the correct phone number, averted disaster, and made a point to really get to know Andrea. The more I learned about her, the more I was attracted to her. I was sad when she had to return to California but there was no way I could follow her back. I had two years left on my professional basketball contract and had to stay in the Philippines. She went back to Long Beach and I remained in Manila but Andrea made a great effort to keep in touch even though this was before the days of Viber, WhatsApp, and Facetime.

The first chance I got to go back to the US was during the offseason in 2004 and all I thought about during that visit was finding a way to ask

Andrea out again. As fate would have it, my cousin was getting married and had asked me to be his best man. Naturally, I needed a date to the wedding so I mustered the courage to ask Andrea if she would accompany me. I was over the moon when she said yes. I still remember how she looked that day—she wore a beautiful green dress that matched her gorgeous green eyes. I didn't want to admit it then, but I think I was already falling in love.

It was not often that I brought a date of mine to meet my parents and relatives and I worried about how my family would react to Andrea. Filipino families are usually very critical of potential significant others. This protective instinct stems from our culture's focus on close-knit family ties. I prayed to Jesus that day even if I didn't fully believe in Him yet. I prayed that there would be no judgment from my family.

To my surprise and relief, everyone accepted Andrea. They were warm and welcoming and appeared to like her as much as I did. I had tortured myself with worry that my family wouldn't receive her well but I had nothing to worry about as it turned out. This is a prime example of the habit I developed of psyching myself out in certain situations. Having the courage to ask Andrea out that summer was one of the first brave things I willed myself to do and it was going so well that I wished it didn't have to end but the magic of my cousin's summer wedding faded and bliss gave way to reality.

Andrea and I were really compatible, no doubt about it. We went to a lot of clubs in the US with friends and my sister, who is a terrific judge of character, and Andrea fit right in as part of the group. It was one of the happiest times of my life. However, I knew that I had a job to return to in Manila and that, if I started a serious relationship with Andrea, I might end up breaking her heart. There were too many temptations in Manila for any young man, let alone a well-known professional basketball player, to resist. I couldn't stand the idea of betraying Andrea in any way so the best thing to do was to let her go. With great sadness, I told her before I went back that I didn't see it working out between us.

Andrea was hurt, I knew, but she put on a brave face and we maintained our friendship during my time in the PBA. I didn't want to forget about her even if that was not the right time for us to be in a romantic relationship. I hadn't broken things off because I didn't want to be with her; I broke them off because I did want to be with her but I wanted to give what we had together the best chance of survival. Trying to make it work long-distance would have caused irreparable damage to something so new. So, Andrea kept in touch and I reluctantly kept my distance.

A while after that summer I spent with Andrea, I began dating the woman I was with at the time of the accident. This woman was considered incredibly desirable by many people in Manila and I was so busy congratulating myself over the fact that she had chosen me that I was able to ignore the fact that my real desire was living in Long Beach. I had forced myself to forget about Andrea as best I could and became focused on trying to resurrect my career, which up to 2006, had been on life support itself. Miraculously, I had been given significant playing time in Purefoods, a championship contender, and things were looking rosy right up to the moment I went for that rebound.

***

A funny thing happened while I was rehabbing at SCI-FIT in California. Andrea drove up to visit me and she was there for one of my therapy sessions. Times had changed since the summer when she had accompanied me to my cousin's wedding but Andrea's presence at the rehabilitation center that day made the session special. It might have been born of my desire to impress her but that visit marked a milestone in my post-paralysis life—I was able to take my first few steps on an anti-gravity treadmill.

A few years went by and Andrea continued to keep in touch and visit. As it turned out, one of the weekends that she had planned to come up to see me coincided with a friend's wedding. Hoping to relive some of the magic of that summer in 2004, I asked Andrea to once again be my date for the wedding. She said yes but, before she visited, she wanted me to know that she had recently given her life to Jesus Christ becoming a born-again Christian and making Jesus the Lord of her life.

***

> *"...He had no stately form or majesty to attract us, no beauty that we should desire Him. He was despised and rejected by men, a man of sorrows, acquainted with grief.*

> *Like one from whom men hide their faces, He was despised, and we esteemed him not. Surely He took up our infirmities and carried our sorrows; yet we considered Him stricken by God, struck down and afflicted. But He was pierced for our transgressions, He was crushed for our iniquities; the punishment that bought us peace was upon him, and by His stripes we are healed."*[20]
>
> -Isaiah 53:2-53:5

This may seem sacrilegious or even blasphemous to say but Jesus was not really that handsome. It is not my intent to be shallow but I believe that this idea is supported by various verses in scripture. There is no doubt that Jesus had a spiritual beauty that attracted people to him but I'm am referring to pure aesthetic beauty at the moment. There are other people in the Bible who are documented as being handsome. Saul, the king that the Israelites yearned for, was said to be being tall, dark, and handsome. Solomon, the son of David, who became the wisest man on the face of the earth--that guy was handsome. I imagine one would need to possess a certain level of handsomeness to have 700 wives and 300 concubines. Those figures, King Saul and King Solomon, are hard for most of us to relate to though.

By contrast, Jesus was documented as having "no stately form or majesty to attract us." He was just a regular guy. That's probably why He was able to fly under the radar for the first few months of His ministry. He was (thank you, Joan Osborne) one of us. Jesus came to us in the most average form possible. He did not set Himself up to be put on a pedestal. He was put on a cross, one of the most shameful means of death in the Roman world. Death by crucifixion was reserved for criminals and the dregs of society and when Jesus was sentenced to that horrible end by Pontius Pilate, we can assume He was not just being put to death, he was being stripped of all dignity.

Think about that the next time you become dissatisfied with your life. When I was paralyzed, I lost my career. I lost the social status and the perks that came with being a professional basketball player. I was no longer the

---

[20] *The Holy Bible: New International Version, NIV.* (Biblica Inc. 1973, 1978, 1984, 2011).

tall guy who could ball. I was just the guy who needed an extra-long bed to lie in day in and day out when I could no longer move. Yet Jesus must have had empathy for me because He suffered the loss of His friends and followers and experienced a great reduction in status as well, going from revered teacher to criminal on a cross.

When He was being beaten and tortured by the Roman soldiers, Jesus must have wished that He did not have to feel the pain of the whips and scourges but He knew He had to endure it because it was God's plan. This was how God intended that He should be able to relate to all of us sinners. "By His stripes we are healed." His stripes—those long wounds inflicted by the whip and borne by our Savior. These were the marks of the *cat-of-nine-tails*, a multi-tailed whip used by the Romans to inflict unbearable pain on the backs of their prisoners.

There is both spiritual and physical significance embedded in these stripes that Jesus bore. According to historians and biblical scholars, the Romans would whip a person a maximum of 39 times. This is likely because the Romans knew, having learned through a process of trial and error, that once the 40th lash was inflicted upon someone, that person was likely to die right then and there. The Romans whipped Jesus 39 times, inflicting upon Him the most pain they could while still leaving Him alive to suffer the even worse pain of death by crucifixion.

Many experts believe that all the diseases in the world can be grouped according to 39 basic categories. Now while many doctors and experts in the field of medicine may react strongly to this assertion, I would like you to consider the implications of this link between the 39 lashes that Jesus bore and the 39 types of diseases in the world. It was pre-determined by God that Jesus should suffer, both figuratively and symbolically, every type of punishment that could be inflicted upon someone. The Creator of the Universe saw it fitting that the Romans would whip Jesus for every type of malady that He Himself created to serve the function of justice.

What this means in layman's terms is that God "took it all out on Him." Jesus's battered body absorbed the entire brunt of this punishment so that we would be washed clean and able start a relationship with a Holy God. The sicknesses and diseases of the world are forms of God's vengeance in a sense. They are punishments created following the expulsion of Adam and Eve from Eden. God inflicted the damage of all the disease He created onto the human body of His only Son. Jesus' death and the pain He suffered shortly before He died are the perfect juxtaposition of both mercy and justice. In order to forgive us of our great debt, God had to make sure that someone paid the price for it in full.

***

The next time you are down in the doldrums and are itching for medication that will calm the stormy waters of your mind, remember that Jesus is the God who empathizes with us. Know that there is no form of suffering so painful that He cannot identify and remedy it. Recall the story of the 39 lashes and how all manner of diseases and ailments were dumped upon Him and take heart in the fact that He knows what you are going through.

I imagine that if someone would have performed a modern-day type of autopsy on the Savior's body after he was brought down from the cross, they would have found physical manifestations of illnesses to fill an entire medical journal. Jesus, right before He died, was a walking text book of physical ailments. He suffered all for us. He experienced the proverbial "world of hurt," was beaten and tortured, because God cared about us so deeply. He spared no expense in "buying" our forgiven state and the price that was paid was enormous indeed.

I know that depression is a real thing and has many causes, some situational and some chemical. Life can place a great deal of stress on us and there are times that we struggle to cope with it. I did a lot of struggling and even considered killing myself so I would never make light of depression or disparage anyone for seeking medical treatment for this condition. What I do wish to illustrate though, is that an eternal perspective can help cure us of our obsession with ourselves and the idea that everything in the world revolves around the pain we feel.

We believe two main lies when we are down in the dumps of depression: First, we believe that our suffering has the power to trap us and hold us in our misery. Secondly, we believe that no one really understands what we are going through because it is just so painful. The truth is, Jesus took on all of our suffering in order for Him to be able to relate to us and to show us that, just as He resurrected from the dead, we also have the same power to move on from our debilitating conditions.

The message of the risen Jesus is not that God inflicted suffering upon his son because he is a sadist. God inflicted this pain so that the contrast of healing and restoration would be even more pronounced. Think of Jesus's followers who couldn't believe their eyes when they encountered Him and He spoke to them as a resurrected person. They just couldn't believe how His wounds had healed! He had healed so much and so completely that He actually looked handsome.

If you are going through, as John of the Cross so aptly named it, the "Dark Night of the Soul," know that there is a God who can turn your mourning into dancing. He is the same God who raised Jesus from the dead because for every form of suffering there is a corresponding form of Healing. God is described in scripture as *Jehovah Rapha*, the God who heals our infirmities. He is the greatest physician we could ever imagine because He not only heals, He also gives brand new life!

***

The most miraculous thing about my healing was not the actual physical healing. In all honesty, I haven't had a good night's sleep since the accident. My back still sends spasms throughout my entire body which cause me to wake up every hour or so. Sometimes, when I am taking care of my twin boys at home, I realize just how broken my body is still, in spite of all the progress I have made. I know that there will be a better body waiting for me in heaven and thank goodness for that because I am not really excited about this one anymore. What I am excited about is the healing that took place in my heart, soul, and spirit.

Since the Lord revealed Himself to me, the burden and weight of trying to be somebody I am not has been lifted off me. I no longer have to be a famous basketball player. I don't have to focus on the fact that my career got cut short in one of the most tragic ways possible. None of that matters to me anymore. What matters to me is that Christ made me whole again with His love. Now, in place of depression and thoughts of suicide, I have dreams of spreading this light that I am experiencing on a daily basis.

I get excited when I think about all the souls who are weary and tired of wearing all those masks that the world expects them to wear. They are going to hear the good news of the Gospel through me! While it is true that what I went through was very painful, it is also true that the God I serve empathizes with me and knows what I felt at the time and what I am feeling right now. He has walked a mile in my shoes and He says to me today, "no longer do you have to carry that burden. You are now free because I suffered and died in your place."

***

Andrea told me before we attended my friend's wedding that she had given her life to the Lord. I didn't quite comprehend what it meant at the time but I did muster up the courage to ask her if she would like to start a relationship with me. To my surprise, this time Andrea rejected me, but she did it for a very specific reason. She told me that she wanted me to get to know Jesus first. She knew the hard road I had been down and the toll the recovery was taking on my mental state. She knew that I needed God to heal me from the inside out before I could seriously think about dating her. To this day, I marvel at her courage for being able to tell me that.

I learned that God "makes all things beautiful in His time"[21] when, a year and a half later, Andrea called me up and asked if I was ready to be in a relationship with her. I couldn't believe my ears. After all the pain I went through, after the sadness of leaving Andrea the first time to go back to the Philippines in 2004, here she was more than a decade later, wanting to continue where we had left off.

Up to that point, I was convinced that my dating life was over. I still tried to date but, deep inside, I believed that no one *really* wanted to be with a quadriplegic. My self-esteem was low and I couldn't see how anyone would willingly sacrifice a portion of their happiness to go through the struggles of life with someone in a wheelchair. It just didn't make any sense. I had been dumped by one girlfriend for being damaged goods yet here Andrea was, offering me the kind of unconditional love that Hollywood romances and date movies don't show enough of.

Being in a wheelchair and recovering from a spinal cord injury are not easy circumstances. I still have a catheter attached to me for when I need to pee. As I mentioned, I don't ever get a good night's sleep because my spine sends electrical shocks to the various parts of my body that wake me

---

[21] Ecclesiastes 3:11, *The Holy Bible: New International Version, NIV* (Biblica Inc. 1973, 1978, 1984, 2011).

up every hour. Any partner of mine would have to put up with all of that. Surely an attractive girl like Andrea, who had only gotten more attractive since I first met her in 2004, didn't need to deal with that drama.

Never the less, Andrea agreed to be my date for a third time at a wedding, only this time it was *our* wedding. I could finally forget the heartache I had experienced when I had let her go years earlier because God had brought us together once more. As I watched her walk down the aisle in her beautiful white dress, tears rolled down my cheeks. I was a broken man, a man with shattered dreams and a shattered spine to match, but here was this person who was willing to walk with me step by step, allowing me to heal with her and to grow with her.

Andrea has never treated me like a charity case. She overlooks my shortcomings, the things I cannot do, and sees the things I can. She encourages me to fulfill my destiny—one that is far greater than any championship glory I could have achieved as a professional basketball player. Andrea has taken my whole being and accepted me for who I am. She loves me no matter what, and in her eyes, it doesn't matter that I am in a wheelchair, or that I am no longer that young man she once met in a bar in Manila while she was vacationing after college graduation. I am the person she loves and this means that she accepts me with each and every one of my faults in mind. She knows about my scars, both the literal ones and the emotional ones. She knows that it broke my heart to hear on national TV that I had "changed" and had become "a monster" but Andrea made me realize that I didn't have to blame myself any longer for what had happened—it was all a part of God's plan to be the kind of person He was raising me up to be.

There were so many emotions coursing through me on that day that Andrea became my wife. I thought about the accident, that moment when I lay on the court believing I had lost everything. I thought about how on this day--my wedding day--God turned my mourning into dancing. I had been angry at Him for many years for the loss of the woman I had been seeing but I realized then that He was just saving me for the right person. As the minister spoke those famous words, "You may now kiss the bride," I said a silent prayer that I would not wake up and find this had all been a dream. It seemed way too good to be true.

I lifted the veil that covered my wife's beautiful green eyes, so full of unconditional love and affection, and I knew that this love would last several lifetimes over. I thought about all the things that this woman had become to me: friend, companion, confidant, lover, inspiration. As I brought myself up to kiss her, I could almost hear the jubilant angels rejoicing in a moment of redemption, reconciliation, and rapture all rolled into one.

CHAPTER 15
"CLOSING WITH THANKS"

It is now 2020 and I am fourteen years removed from my accident. Once again, we just celebrated Mother's Day and my mind drifts to what it was like that night when my spine shattered and my dreams for the life I thought I was going to have lay wasted around me. I have so much more now than I ever would have thought possible. Even if I am in a wheelchair, I can actually walk for certain distances and I am not confined to a bed. I am able to drive, so much so that a ride sharing program trusts me with the safety of its passengers. I have a beautiful wife and two wonderful twin boys, and I believe in the possibility that God might bless us with more children in the future. When I look back on the journey, I realize that my heart is filled with gratitude for so many things.

***

"Consider it pure joy, my brothers and sisters, whenever you face trials of many kinds, because you know that the testing of your faith produces perseverance. Let perseverance finish its work so that you may be mature and complete, not lacking anything."
-James 1:2-4, New International Version

"Dear friends, don't be surprised at the fiery trials you are going through, as if something strange were happening to you. Instead, be very glad—for these trials make you partners with

> *Christ in His suffering, so that you will have the wonderful joy of seeing His glory when it is revealed to all the world."*[22]
> -1 Peter 4:12-4:13

I hope you have learned in reading this book that, even in our darkest moments, we must always be thankful! Gratitude for our blessings in times of strife help us overcome the "fight or flight" response caused by primal fear that leads us to make poor decisions and make us blind to possibility. Gratitude is a powerful tool that people can use daily to change the world for the better. After fourteen years of living through and with this crazy paralysis, I can sum it up with one thought: I am thankful for my injury and suffering because it made me more like my Savior, Jesus, and I can only change the world if I am more like Him.

I believe we have been deluded into thinking that life should be about being comfortable. Life is about the development of our character and our constant internal growth. It is about the refinement of our spirits. More often than not, we have to go through varying degrees of pain and suffering in order to realize the kind of treasure that God has in store for us. I sincerely believe that the point of life is to love the Lord and serve others and sometimes that means getting a little uncomfortable.

Those who followed Jesus when he was on Earth, who heard the gospel first hand, were not seeking comfort. They traveled far and wide, leaving their homes and families behind for life spent on dusty roads and in inhospitable towns. They risked hunger and exposure to the elements and, in some cases, deaths as brutal as their master's death. The apostle Peter was crucified upside down some 30 odd years after Jesus was crucified. Why should we find encouragement in that? It is a reminder that it is not a hoarded treasure in this life that will bring us everlasting peace but the treasure of eternal life in Christ!

I can attest that I was once blinded by the earthly returns this world offers. I thought I had it figured out. I'd take names and kick ass on the basketball court, sign three or four large paydays, retire, and possibly put up a nightclub or bar after retirement. Yet when I consider all that I have gone through these past fourteen years, I would never trade any of it for

---

[22] 1 Peter 4:12-4:13 *The Holy Bible: New Living Translation.* (Tyndale House Foundation, 1996, 2004, 2015).

that "other" dream. That is an absolute revelation from God. It is easy to be grateful when life is going well but we can also be extremely grateful as we go through the worst trials and setbacks. Often times, the trials and setbacks are blessings in disguise. Little did I know that my paralysis was the start of the abundant life God had in store for me.

***

I recently came upon a song by the band *I am They*. The song is called "Scars"[23] and it talks about why we can be thankful even if we have gone through something truly horrific.

> *Darkest water and deepest pain*
> *I wouldn't trade it for anything*
> *Cause my brokenness*
> *brought me to you*
> *and these wounds are a story you'll use.*

Having my ability to make a living taken from me was something I was not prepared for in any way. I spent countless nights cursing God, cursing myself, and blaming others because of what had befallen me. My thoughts were always, *if only that had not happened, I would be living a great life just like my friends who are still in the league.* All the while I was sitting on this great opportunity to share my story. I just did not have the right attitude at the time to see the new path God had set down for me when the roadblock went up on the path I thought I was supposed to travel.

God gave me new insight to change the way I view my accident. Looking back, I really would not trade what happened for anything because the brokenness and the process of being brought low carried me closer to God. Before that, God might as well have been some magical genie to whom I would run if I needed money or something. I had never considered that life actually revolved around Him and that I was called to be a part of His kingdom.

---

[23] Ethan Hulse, Jon McConnel, Matthew Armstrong, Matthew Hein. "Scars," *Scars*, performed by I am They. Essential Records, 2018.

The paralysis did so much for me, giving as much as it took and more. It humbled me and allowed me to stop comparing myself to other people. It enabled me to focus on the things I had instead of the things I could have or thought I should have. It taught me to stop letting external circumstances affect my own inner peace

> *So I'm thankful for the scars*
> *Cause without them I wouldn't know your heart*
> *And I know they'll always tell of who you are*
> *So forever I am thankful for the scars.*

It is easy to read these lyrics when the scars are little but it is harder to believe the message when your whole body has become a scarred-over wound and a battleground that shocks you awake every hour every night for fourteen years. After the numerous surgeries and treatments I received and the painstaking work it took to get back to walking again with the use of crutches, I have made my peace with the lyrics of this song. If I can, so can you.

What is God's heart? What is His deepest wish for us? It is not for us to get rich—this is not some multi-level marketing program I'm trying to recruit you into. God's wish is for us to be more like Him. It is to embody His love as fully as we can here on Earth. It is for us to encourage the downtrodden. God's heart is a leader and a servant and compels us to lift up those who are weak. There is an old Sunday School song that comes to mind when I think about God's heart:

> *Make me a servant*
> *Humble and meek*
> *Lord let me lift up those who are weak*
> *And may the prayer of my heart always be*
> *'Make me a servant today.'*[24]

After my accident, I realized that I had been focusing on the wrong things. I had it backwards all along. I was not put on this earth to exalt

---

[24] Willard, Kelly Willard. "Make Me A Servant." Maranatha Music/Willing Heart Music/CCCM, 1982.

myself and live the lifestyle of the rich and famous. I was put on this earth to serve others and to do my best imitation of Christ. Referring back to the song "Scars" by I am They:

> *Now I'm standing in confidence*
> *With the strength of your faithfulness*
> *And I'm not who I was before*
> *No, I don't have to fear anymore.*

It is profound and amazing that I am now standing with confidence. In the months after the accident of May 2006, I was in a worse state than Denzel Washington's character, the brilliant cop Lincoln Rhyme, in *The Bone Collector*, one of my favorite movies. He could only move his right pointer finger (although he still managed to kick ass and solve crimes) and I could not move anything below my neck. The doctors, as well-meaning as they were, tried to temper my expectations by reminding me that I only had a 4% chance of ever walking again—aka a 96% chance of NEVER walking again. I was not going to be able to play basketball again, just when my market value was at its highest. There was no Brinks Truck coming with a stack of cash but there were thousands upon thousands of dollars in hospital expenses adding up. Then add in, on top of all that, my girlfriend leaving me for another man in the most embarrassing way possible. It was a lot to say the least.

Taking all the above into consideration, you can see why I might have considered life not worth living but there were so many things that God had in store for me in the coming 13 years that I didn't anticipate. He changed my physical circumstances and was able to change my heart and soul as well. He can do the same for you if you let Him. As this book draws to a close and there are a few points that I'd like to share in the hopes that they might help you on your journey to a better understanding of how God can work miracles in your life.

> **1.) Stop Comparing Yourself to Others.** One of the reasons I was so upset about the accident initially was because, not only was I losing out on a giant PBA contract, I was losing out on the opportunity to compete with my close circle of friends. There had always been

a (mostly) friendly spirit of competition between us and these men all went on to have very long and successful careers in pro basketball. When I considered where I was and where they were, it was hard not be jealous. They were accomplishing all the goals I had set for myself while I was bound to a wheelchair. I believed I would never have the chance to prove my worth the way they were doing.

No matter what country you live in or what your socioeconomic status is, chances are you can relate to the concept of keeping up with the Joneses. No matter how blessed we are, there is always going to be someone who has more than we do and it is tempting to covet the other person's fortunes but, the moment our happiness depends on a favorable comparison to others, we set a very dangerous precedent. Believing that our self-worth is based on our performance ability or on our income is a lie that will lead us to misery.

I did not truly become happy until I decided to focus on running my own race. We each have our own path in life with our own specific challenges to face and we can't compare our progress with someone else's. I learned that there was a special purpose and a special mission for me to fulfill beyond the basketball court and I stopped focusing on how much better off others were than I was. Once I did that, I was able to be truly happy for them and happy for myself as well.

2.) **Focus on What You Have and Not on What You Don't.** The lie that we always need more and that there is no such thing as enough is a destructive weapon designed to keep us constantly working for things that we don't really want or need. If you have a roof over your head, are eating three times a day, and have access to running water, you are in the 95th percentile of the world's richest people and are truly blessed.

So many of us go around feeling empty inside because we constantly think only of the things that we don't have. We need to reframe our thinking entirely. Don't have a car? Thank the Lord that you are able to walk to the subway station with your own two legs! Don't have a fancy house? Be thankful for the living space you do have that protects you from the elements! Don't have a vacation getaway spot? Be thankful for the wonders of your immediate surroundings right now! The grass isn't always greener on the other side and these times we are living in now will eventually be the "good old days" of tomorrow! Be present in the moment and think about all the things you have and be thankful for them.

3.) Do Not Let External Circumstances Affect Your Inner Peace. Have you ever met an unhappy person? I have. I used to meet him every day when I looked in the mirror. Now when I see my reflection, I am reminded of that unhappy person who used to inhabit my body and can proudly state, "Not anymore!" I am free today because I realized that my inner peace cannot be affected by anyone but me. Unhappy people love to blame others and spread their negative energy around like wildfire. The next time you encounter one of these people, try to move as far away as possible! And if that negative person is you, focus on changing the thing inside you that is always looking for something to be unhappy about.

We do not need to be successful in order to be happy; we do, however, need to be happy in order to be successful! By refusing to let any circumstance affect the joy we feel in the wellspring of our hearts, we are making the decision to be thankful and happy today. I believe that gratitude is greater than fear and freedom from fear means being able to rejoice in our present state and to envision and take hold of the glorious future ahead of us.

***

I would like to thank you for taking the time to read this simple book. There is much to my story that I didn't go into on these pages but I tried to focus on the major elements and the parts of my journey that I believe would be the most useful to you. After all, that is my purpose here on earth: I am here to serve you and I hope my message will benefit you. Please remember that having an attitude of gratitude leaves a lasting impact on our minds and bodies. We can transform ourselves just by changing our default state from a negative one to a much more positive one. When we are thankful in all things, God will be able to use us to accomplish the great things He has in store for all of humanity.

There are some people that I would like to thank before I sign off. Aside from the people I spoke of in Chapter 11, there were key men and women who reminded me that followers of Jesus Christ do not transform in isolation. We all need to heal in the context of community. These were the people who became my community and whose assistance set me a on path towards healing my soul and giving me purpose.

The first of these special people was Alex Compton. Alex was a professional basketball player in the Philippines who went on to be one of the best head coaches in the country. Alex was the first person to call me a "world changer" and he believed in my ability to use my unique platform even if it took me more than a decade to believe in it myself. Alex prophesied that I would one day have a large impact on millions of people. He said he always knew that I was more than just a basketball player and I am so thankful for the love and support he has shown me.

The second person I want to acknowledge is Tony de la Cruz. In 2012 I returned to Manila. It had been six years since my paralysis and I still didn't know how to go about sharing my story on a broader stage. Then I ran into Tony, a fellow Fil-American basketball player. Tony and I had not been that close when I was playing in the league but we became reacquainted on my return visit and it was Tony who gave me key ideas on how to spread my message. Through him, I was able to connect with my co-author on this project and I was able to get a head start on speaking in public forums.

Tony's many connections enabled me to land a few speaking engagements with some top Philippine corporations. During one event, I spoke with top-level managers-in-training and, although I had practiced my speech many times, I wasn't prepared for the reaction of the audience. I had touched on the concept of using adversity to propel us forward. I talked about defying the odds and strategic risk. I ended the speech by rising from my wheelchair and standing. I was still shaky on my feet and had to use the help of walking sticks but I looked up and saw tears. There was not a dry eye in sight.

Tony believed in my abilities even when I didn't. Even if Alex Compton made the initial prophecy in terms of my becoming a speaker, it was Tony and his vision and connections that gave me the confidence I needed to make that prophecy a reality. While he may humbly downplay his contributions to my newfound calling in life, I believe God sent Tony to show me that I could accomplish much more than I ever dreamt of as a basketball player.

Rob Johnson was another Filipino-American professional basketball player who had a great impact on my journey to where I am today. He gave up a life of fame and prestige as a professional baller to become a pastor in the Philippines. Rob made sure that I was spiritually taken care during those rough patches in my life when I didn't really feel like getting to know God. Through his fervent prayers and honest talks with me, I was able to understand the messages God was sending me. Rob helped me understand scripture and loved me in the way that the Bible commands us to love one another. I am thankful that he took the time to travel part of this rough road with me.

My list of thanks would not be complete without Anne Espiritu who used to drive me to church in the US when the last thing I wanted to do was attend. In the days after my paralysis, all I wanted to do was to sit at home and wallow in self-pity but Anne took the time to drive me, to bring me to church, and to minister to me by telling me the truth of God's love in my life. She pointed me to the cross and she helped me understand that the Lord was not done transforming my mind, body, and spirit. I will forever be grateful for Anne as I would not have been able to achieve the spiritual breakthroughs I achieved if it were not for her consistent presence during my darkest times.

Last but not least, there was Debra Amour. Debra worked with my mother as a nurse at Seton Medical Center in Daly City, California. She approached my mom one day and said that she was a healer and someone who believed in New Age philosophies. While I may not necessarily believe in all of that as a Christian, I do believe that God used Debra to reach me.

When I was trying to walk again in the early stages of my recovery in the US, Debra became like a therapist, talking me through overcoming the darkness I was feeling. She taught me how to meditate and how to be still. I wasn't a Christian yet when she taught me these techniques but the amazing thing was, in one meditation, I heard a voice saying: "I am the one healing you. I am the one who makes all things new." I believe this was the voice of Jesus Himself and I immediately turned to the Bible to look for answers after hearing that voice.

I sought to know the Lord and I changed my meditation from just an exercise to a time of communion and prayer with Jesus. I was able to use the techniques taught to me by Debra to be still before God and to let His goodness wash over me. Every time I feel stressed to this day, I close my eyes and think about the peace that came to me when I was at my worst. This is the kind of peace that is available to all of us today. Jesus is calling to us and telling us that true happiness and joy are to be found only in Him.

This leads me to the final and most important point I want to share with you. I want you to know that true happiness and joy are gifts you can have right now if you choose. True joy, the real and lasting kind--the kind that makes us eternally safe and secure and free from any fear or worries that the world may place on us--may be found if you turn your heart and mind to Jesus. He is standing at the door of your heart, waiting patiently for you to admit that you need Him. At the end of the day, all of us will die. While I have made a recovery from paralysis, one day my soul will have to leave this mortal coil that wraps it. One day I will cross from this life into eternity and what I have made of my life here on earth will have eternal ramifications. I am confident that when I choose to place my faith in God and His son, Jesus Christ, I have chosen the path of blessings and hope which leads to eternal joy and peace.

If you haven't made the decision regarding whom to place your faith in yet, and if you want to be certain about spending eternity in the arms of our loving Savior, the One who heals all wounds, I'd like you to pray this prayer with me now. It is a Prayer of Salvation, Eugene Tejada Style.

> Lord Jesus, thank you for saving me.
> Thank you for dying on the cross for our sins.
> You took those whips to the back like a champion
> and resisted the urge to condemn your persecutors,
> crying out, "Father forgive them for they know not what they do!"
> You suffered all this because you loved us.

So now I come to you asking for your forgiveness for myself.
I have lived my life with the wrong set of priorities.
I didn't know that the secret to true joy lies in you.
Help me be connected to that source of true Joy.
Please come into my heart today and be the Lord of my life.

There are so many mistakes that I've made.
I've messed up and I've fallen short of your standard.
Help me to be more like you in every way.
I know you won't be done changing me until the day I die,
but I am asking you to change me from glory to glory.
Change me a little at a time,
as much as you are willing to be patient.
I put my complete trust in You.

Nothing I do or have ever done can merit my salvation.
You alone are the bridge that allows me to cross over from death to life.
You are the one who can turn paralysis to liberation.
You raise me up when I am unable to stand.
You take my delicate carcass of a body and
transform it into something new.
You lift me up out of the miry pit and cause me to rejoice.
It is the kind of joy that can never be taken away because
it is the joy that comes from You.

You are the key to the Father and you are the
reason I can be reconciled with Him.
I will always be a sinner but because I am covered by your blood,
the Father looks at me as a saint.
Help me to enjoy you always and to abide in you always.
I make this life-changing decision today.
I love you, Lord.

In Jesus' mighty Name I sincerely pray,
Amen.

Manufactured by Amazon.ca
Bolton, ON